GLOBETROTTER™
Travel Guide

LISBON AND PORTUGAL

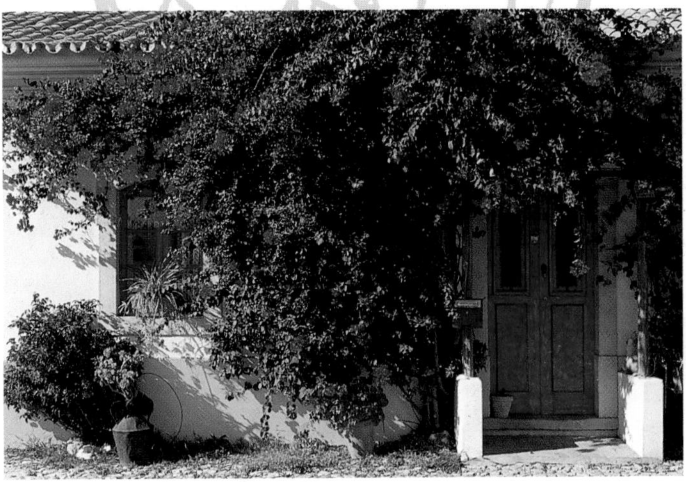

JANE O'CALLAGHAN

NEW
HOLLAND

★★★	Highly recommended
★★	Recommended
★	See if you can

Third edition published in 2009
by New Holland Publishers (UK) Ltd
London • Cape Town • Sydney • Auckland
10 9 8 7 6 5 4 3 2 1
website: www.newhollandpublishers.com

Garfield House, 86 Edgware Road
London W2 2EA, United Kingdom

80 McKenzie Street
Cape Town 8001, South Africa

Unit 1, 66 Gibbes Street, Chatswood,
NSW 2067, Australia

218 Lake Road, Northcote,
Auckland, New Zealand

Distributed in the USA by
The Globe Pequot Press, Connecticut

ISBN 978 1 84773 296 5

This guidebook has been written by independent
authors and updaters. The information therein
represents their impartial opinion, and neither they
nor the publishers accept payment in return for
including in the book or writing more favourable
reviews of any of the establishments. Whilst every
effort has been made to ensure that this guidebook
is as accurate and up to date as possible, please
be aware that the facts quoted are subject to
change, particularly the price of food, transport
and accommodation. The Publisher accepts no
responsibility or liability for any loss, injury or
inconvenience incurred by readers or travellers
using this guide.

Publishing Manager: Thea Grobbelaar
DTP Cartographic Manager: Genené Hart
Editors: Nicky Steenkamp, Alicha van Reenen,
Tarryn Berry
Picture Researcher: Shavonne Govender
Design and DTP: Nicole Bannister, Éloïse Moss
Cartographers: Inga Ndibongo, Nicole Bannister
Reproduction by Resolution (Cape Town) and Hirt &
Carter (Pty) Ltd, Cape Town.
Printed and bound by Times Offset (M) Sdn. Bhd.,
Malaysia.

Photographic Credits:
Paul Bernhardt: title page, pages 17, 18, 23, 24, 25,
26 (left), 36, 40, 41, 42, 52, 55, 62, 69, 112, 115,
116; **Justin Fox:** page 16; **International
PhotoBank/Adrian Baker:** page 67; **International
PhotoBank/Peter Baker:** pages 4, 7, 9, 21, 27, 28,
46, 54, 86, 96, 107; **Caroline Jones:** pages 14, 34,
35, 60, 66, 70, 72, 80; **David Mace:** pages 8, 10, 11,
12, 13, 15, 38, 43, 51, 56, 57, 63, 64, 65, 68, 71,
73, 74, 75, 76, 77, 82, 83, 84, 85, 87, 88, 89, 90,
91, 92, 93, 103; **Jane O'Callaghan:** pages 22, 33, 48,
53, 104, 105; **Photo Access/4cornersimage.com/
Johanna Huber:** page 6; **Pictures Colour Library:**
cover; **Neil Setchfield:** pages 20, 26 (right), 29, 30,
37, 98, 99, 100, 110, 113, 114, 117, 119, 120.

Keep us Current
Information in travel guides is apt to change, which
is why we regularly update our guides. We'd be
grateful to receive feedback if you've noted something we should include in our updates. If you have
new information, please share it with us by writing to
the Publishing Manager, Globetrotter, at the office
nearest to you (addresses on this page). The most
significant contribution to each new edition will
receive a free copy of the updated guide.

Cover: A view of Arco Triunfal, Praça do Comércio,
Lisbon.
Title Page: Typical Algarve vernacular architecture.

CONTENTS

1
Introducing
Lisbon and Portugal

Portugal sits on the edge of Europe; the westernmost point of the continent is marked by a sheer cliff north of Lisbon. The mighty **Atlantic Ocean** which washes the shores has shaped the country's history from the earliest days. Its presence inspired Portugal's push to discover new lands in the 15th century and opened the country to seaborne traders and conquerors before the Christian era.

Despite being physically isolated from the rest of Europe, Portugal is anything but inward-looking. **Maritime contact** with other seafaring nations over thousands of years has shaped the modern nation. This continuous familiarity with other cultures makes it a very rewarding destination to visit. Overseas visitors are welcomed and their strange customs tolerated. **Hospitality** is just one of the old-fashioned virtues which flourish in Portugal.

Portugal is a relatively small country – less than three-quarters of the size of England – and is easy to explore from the brooding northern **mountains** to the sunny **beaches** of the Algarve, with a fascinating collection of historical sites en route. As well as medieval churches and castles you'll find lovely **gardens**, dramatic **dolmens** and stunning **painted tiles** which seem to decorate every available flat surface. Good roads and inexpensive car hire make touring simple; there's also a reasonable public transport system. Whatever your interests – **history**, **art**, **wine**, playing **golf** on championship courses, relaxing in some of the most bucolic **rural landscapes** in Europe, or simply soaking up the sunshine – enjoy, and as the locals say, *boa viagem*, meaning 'have a good journey'.

TOP ATTRACTIONS

*** Lisbon: spend some time sightseeing in the historic and exciting capital.
*** Sintra: immerse yourself in the romance and history of this lovely town.
*** Évora: Neolithic remains, Roman ruins and a medieval old town make this a must.
** Oporto and surroundings: start in the city and then explore the historic wine-growing regions of the Minho and Douro.
** Algarve: millions of happy sun worshippers and golfers can't be wrong.

Opposite: *A winning smile from a Madeiran girl in traditional costume.*

Above: *Sandy beaches are a feature of the coastline; this fine example is at Praia da Rocha in the Algarve.*

THE LAND

Portugal is slightly dwarfed by its mighty neighbour **Spain,** almost six times as large, but the landscape is just as diverse, if not more so. If you're arriving from the **arid heartland** of Spain you can't help but notice how much lusher, **greener** and prettier the countryside appears. As a general rule of thumb, altitude decreases from the Spanish border to the Atlantic, and from the north to the south.

The oldest rocks, hard granite and shale, sweep in a semicircle from the north along the eastern frontier to the southwest. The emergence of the Alps and Pyrenees forced the primeval **plateau** upwards, fissuring it along fault lines. Associated **volcanic activity** created isolated ranges such as the **Serra de Sintra** and the **Serra de Monchique**. The rivers, Tagus and Sado, drain alluvial basins while secondary limestone deposits are found in a band stretching from Coimbra to Setúbal, and also in the Algarve.

Rivers and Coasts

All the country's main rivers have their source in Spain. The longest is the **Douro,** which crosses Portugal through a series of gorges for 320km (199 miles). Other important rivers are the **Tagus** (Tejo), **Sado**, **Guadiana** and **Mondego**. The Tagus forms a useful marker as it divides the mountainous north from the plateaux and plains of the south. The estuaries of the Tagus and Sado form fine natural **harbours** which have been renowned since pre-Roman times. Portugal has 837km (520 miles) of coastline, mostly west-facing, comprising cliffs, sandbars, sheltered bays and long smooth sweeps of sand. The offshore waters are cooled by a deep-water current from the Canaries.

The Regions

Portugal is composed of **ten** ancient **provinces**, which have been subdivided into administrative districts. **Madeira** and the **Azores** are autonomous regions.

The **Minho** (districts: Braga and Viana do Castelo) and **Douro** (district: Oporto) are largely composed of granite hills covered with dense vegetation and interspersed with the poorer soils of schist outcrops. High rainfall has contributed to intense agricultural activity and a relatively dense population, apart from the wild slopes of the **Peneda-Gerês.**

Trás-os-Montes (districts: Bragança and Vila Real) means 'beyond the mountains' and is an area of high plateaux and hills known as '*terra fria*' (cold land), isolated villages and more sheltered fertile river valleys, including the **Alto Douro** (upper Douro). Here in the '*terra quente*' (hot land) vines, olives, figs and almonds flourish.

Beira Alta (districts: Guarda and Viseu) is the most mountainous region of Portugal, reaching its climax in the 1993m (6539ft) peak of **Torre** in the **Serra da Estrela.** Geographically the province is a western extension of the central **Spanish cordilleras;** the lower mountain slopes are wooded while villagers grow maize and rye in the

ALMOND TIME

The almond tree was brought to the Algarve by the Moors and its delightful white blossoms cover the countryside in February. It was introduced, so the legends go, by a Moorish king who wished to please his Viking bride who was pining for the snows of her native land. He planted the land around the castle with almond trees so that once a year she would feel at home, surrounded by drifts of snowy white blossom.

Below: *The Rio Minho marks the northern frontier with Spain; this view is at Valença, which was once fortified against military incursions from the north.*

PENEDA-GERÊS

Portugal's only **national park** is Peneda-Gerês in the Minho, an area of outstanding natural beauty. The southerly region around the Serra do Gerês is accessible and commercialized; the northern area around the Serra da Peneda is remote and much quieter. Visit the park information office in **Braga** or **Caldas do Gerês** before you go to plan your routes. Walking and riding are the best ways to enjoy the natural scenery but there are relatively few marked trails. There are some bus routes between villages but it's easier to explore the whole region by car. You're unlikely to see the wolves and eagles which still hunt here but if you are fortunate, you may spot roe deer, wild boar, hawks and otters.

Below: *Farms, such as these in Aljezur, tend to be small concerns rather than large-scale operations.*

valleys and graze sheep and goats in the uplands. Neighbouring **Beira Baixa** (district: Castelo Branco) is an eroded plateau dropping towards the Tagus valley, while **Beira Litoral** (districts: Coimbra and Aveiro) is well watered and wooded with long sandy beaches on the coast. Along the shores grow pine trees which stabilize the shifting sand dunes.

Estremadura (districts: Leira, Lisbon and Setúbal) once marked the southern frontier between Christian and Moorish Portugal, hence the name. Here gentle hills punctuate fertile farmland; the coast varies between cliffs, salt marshes, lagoons and sandy bays. **Ribatejo** (district: Santarém), on the banks of the Tagus, is Portugal's agricultural heartland with rice fields, wheat and extensive grass fields where fine horses and bulls for the arena are raised. The plains merge seamlessly with the **Alto** (Upper) **Alentejo** (districts: Évora and Portalegre) and **Baixa** (Lower) **Alentejo** (district: Beja) where the progressively drier and hotter climate produces a landscape similar to the Spanish mesas, with rough grazing and wheat fields interspersed with cork oak and olive groves.

The shales and schists of the **Serra do Caldeirão,** a low range of hills which barely exceeds 500m (1640ft), nevertheless shelter the **Algarve** (district: Faro) from intemperate northern weather. Inland the province is composed of limestone and sandstone hills with Mediterranean-style cultivation in the valleys. The coast varies between the western cliffs with sheltered sandy bays at their foot and the low-lying sandbars of the east.

Climate

There are three major influences at work here: the **Atlantic Ocean**, the continental extremes of the **Spanish interior** and the **Mediterranean**. Much of the north has an Atlantic climate – mild, rainy and changeable. In summer you can expect near-perfect temperatures of around 25°C (77°F) on the coast; inland in the Upper Douro valley the daytime maximum can often exceed 40°C (104°F). Winters are mild on the coast but temperatures drop

below freezing inland, and there is enough **snow** to support ski slopes on the Serra da Estrela. Rainfall varies between 2540mm (100in) annually on exposed hills and as little as 500mm (20in) on the lee slopes to the east.

In central Portugal the climate is transitional between an Atlantic and Mediterranean type, with more Continental influences inland. In general you can expect long hot summers and mild rainy winters. But weather patterns are unpredictable, particularly at the beginning and end of a season; May and October can be either glorious or marked by incessant rain. Having said that, Lisboans frequently enjoy Christmas on the beach. The **Baixa Alentejo** regularly records the highest temperatures in Portugal as well as the lowest rainfall; winters are short and crisp.

The sheltered **Algarve** enjoys hot summers and short mild winters with some 3000 hours of sunshine annually. The south coast has one of the best winter climates in Europe; while it may not be hot enough to sunbathe (although sometimes it is), you should at least be able to enjoy a game of tennis or golf in shirt sleeves, or sit outdoors at a restaurant. In general terms, you can expect most of the rain throughout the country to fall between October and March. Wet weather is associated with Atlantic low pressure systems and when it does rain, it can do so for days.

Above: *Southern Portugal's mild winter climate makes it possible to enjoy the beaches (this fine example is at Estoril) all year round.*

CLIMATE

When to visit depends on your holiday plans. If sightseeing and touring are priorities, avoid high summer anywhere south of Lisbon or you could struggle in temperatures of up to 40°C (104°F). If on the other hand soaking up the sun is a priority you'll find the best weather throughout the country from June to September. Spring and autumn are more equable but also more changeable. Winter temperatures range from a pleasant daytime average maximum of 17°C (62°F) in the Algarve to close to freezing inland in the landlocked northeast. The north, particularly the coast and mountains, is wetter than the south.

Right: *Cistus (rockrose) flourishes in the southern hills and makes a lovely display.*
Opposite: *Tall buildings in quiet surroundings are ideal locations for storks to rear their brood. The pair return to the nest every spring.*

Flora

Portugal's vegetation is a mix of Mediterranean and northern European species, with the proportion varying from north to south. In the north are **deciduous woods** of oak, chestnut, maple, birch and pine, as well as **moors** covered with heather, bracken and cistus (rock rose) at altitude. South of the Tagus **holm** and **cork oaks** prevail, particularly in the Alentejo. Portugal is the world's leading producer of cork. In the Algarve you will find **maquis,** the typical drought-resistant Mediterranean scrub vegetation, known in Portugal as *matos*. Aromatic herbs such as rosemary, lavender, sage and thyme flourish. The Moors introduced carob, almond, fig, orange and lemon trees, which all thrive here. **Eucalyptus plantations** can be found throughout the country. These fast-growing trees, which are cultivated for the paper industry, are detested by environmentalists as not only do they siphon off a great deal of ground water, but they also fail to provide the right habitat for native birds, insects and other animals.

If you're a lover of **wild flowers,** you should visit in the spring. In February the Algarve sees yellow celandine, bermuda buttercups and mimosa bloom beneath the pink and white almond blossom. The blaze of colour sweeps northwards and in March and April pink, blue and scarlet pimpernels, irises, rock roses and poppies appear. Daffodils, camelias and rhododendrons do particularly well in the north. In late spring look out

CORK OAKS

Wherever you go in southern Portugal you'll see these distinctive trees, often with the bark stripped from the trunk. It takes 20 years fora tree to mature sufficiently to become productive; the bark is then stripped every nine years. A tree can live 100 years or more. The number painted on the tree indicates when it was last harvested. Portugal produces over half of the world's cork and if you want to help the environment you should avoid plastic wine stoppers. Cork oak farming is sustainable agriculture at its best and the oak woods provide food for wild animals and birds, shelter from the blazing sun and also the acorns which give the free-range local pork its distinctive taste.

for oleander, gladioli, orchids, tulips and purple jacaranda. The further off the beaten track you travel, the more impressive the spectacle. Pesticides are not yet used in great quantities on smallholdings, and farming methods in some cases have not changed much since medieval times. This passive approach to cultivation allows wild plants to flourish.

Fauna

Most of Portugal's larger mammals have been hunted to extinction. Isolated packs of **wolves** survive along the Spanish border in remote mountain regions. Despite the success of local organization Grupo Lobo in gaining them legal protection they are still shot or poisoned. **Lynx** are confined to the Serra da Malcata (literally 'Bad Cat Mountains', a clue to how these magnificent animals are perceived) in Beira Alta. The Iberian lynx is one of the rarest mammals in Europe. **Wild boar** and red and fallow **deer** are found in the north and east, many on private hunting reserves. Foxes, rabbits and hares are widespread. Of the **reptiles**, lizards and geckoes thrive in the south and the only (mildly) venomous snake is the adder.

Birds of prey include griffon, Egyptian and black vultures, eagles, kites, hawks and owls. You have more chance of seeing them in the **Alentejo** and remote northern areas. **Storks** are a common sight in many parts. Interesting species include bee eaters, hoopoes and bustards. **Flamingos** winter in the Algarve and the Sado estuary. The **Ria Formosa Natural Park** in the Algarve is one of the best places to view waterfowl. Migrating birds overfly the west coast in spring and autumn, with many falling victim to the hunters' guns. Walkers should be aware that the hunting season extends from October to March. Hunters literally shoot anything that moves and their targets are as likely to be their own dogs, tiny songbirds, stray cats and protected species as game.

WILDLIFE HABITATS

These range from mountain areas to estuaries, stretches of coastline and swamps.
National parks: Peneda-Gerês (Minho).
Nature reserves: Montesinho (Trás-os-Montes); Douro Internacional (Trás-os-Montes), Serra da Estrela (Beira Alta); Serras de Aire e Candeeiros (Estremadura); Sintra-Cascais (Estremadura); Serra da Arrábida (Estremadura); Serra de São Mamede (Alto Alentejo); Ria Formosa (Algarve).
Conservation areas: Serra de Malcata (Beira Alta); Paul de Arzila (Beira Litoral); Paul de Boquilobo (Ribatejo); Tagus and Sado estuaries (Estremadura); Sudoeste Alentejano e Costa Vicentina (Alentejo/Algarve coast); Castro Marim (Algarve).

Below: *The design of this hayloft near Estorninhos has remained unchanged for thousands of years.*

HISTORY IN BRIEF
Early History
Portugal has been inhabited since at least 7000BC and had built up a **Neolithic** culture, marked by beehive huts, hill forts, dolmens and passage graves, by 1000BC. Celts moved into the Iberian Peninsula in the 1st millennium BC, at about the same time that trading Phoenicians, Greeks and Carthaginians were visiting southern Portugal. Olisipo, the ancient name for Lisbon, is most probably **Phoenician.**

Arrival of the Romans
After the second Punic War (218–201BC) against the Carthaginians the Roman Empire took over the Iberian Peninsula and Portugal became part of the province of **Hispania Ulterior.** The legions met strong resistance from a Celtic federation of tribes, the **Lusitanians**, who had absorbed and developed the native culture and built hilltop forts known as *castros*. The Lusitanian leader, **Viriatus**, is a celebrated figure in Portuguese folklore in much the same way that Boadicea is in British. Unlike Boadicea, his efforts were successful enough to stop the advance of Rome in its tracks for years; unable to defeat him in battle, the Romans paid to have him murdered in 140BC. **Decimus Junius Brutus** established Olisipo as the capital and advanced on the Douro to secure the north.

But it was **Julius Caesar** who really established Portugal as an integrated part of the Roman Empire in the 1st century BC, founding colonies in Santarém, Beja, Évora, Mértola and Braga. Portugal can still trace its Roman antecedents in its language, roads, legal system and *latifundia* – huge agricultural estates which survive in the Alentejo.

Swabians, Visigoths and Moors
After the fall of the Roman Empire the power vacuum was filled by the Germanic **Swabians** and then the **Visigoths,** Romanized

Christians from eastern France and Germany. In AD711 **Moors** from North Africa crossed the Straits of Gibraltar and met with little resistance from the local population, who had become alienated from their nominal rulers through weak government and religious persecution. Within a decade they held all of Portugal south of the Mondego River, on whose banks Coimbra is located.

As in neighbouring **Andalucía**, the warm land of the Algarve was the Moorish stronghold and **Silves** was the regional capital. At its peak the city was likened to Baghdad, a centre of opulent architecture and scholarship when the rest of Europe was languishing in the Dark Ages. The Moors were tolerant and civilized, and this was a stable and prosperous time for the majority of the population. **Agricultural methods** improved and new crops such as cotton, oranges, lemons, almonds and rice were introduced. Most of the Moors were Berbers from Morocco but Egyptians and Yemenites also settled in the south.

Above: *Azulejos (traditional tiles) decorate the exterior as well as the interior of many buildings; this example is the 18th-century palace of Estói, near Faro.*

HISTORICAL CALENDAR

c2000BC Neolithic settlements in hill forts.
c700BC Celts arrive in the north, Phoenicians in the south.
210BC Romans occupy southern Portugal.
AD410 Germanic Swabians and Visigoths arrive in Portugal.
AD711 Berbers from North Africa and their Arab allies invade and conquer the southern half of the country in seven years.
1143 Afonso Henriques recognized as first king of Portucale.

1249 Reconquest of Portugal completed.
1385 Invading Castilian army beaten at battle of Aljubarrota; start of the Avis dynasty.
1418 Henry the Navigator initiates voyages of discovery.
1498 Vasco da Gama lands in India.
1580 Portugal is annexed by Spain.
1640 Independence restored; start of the Bragança dynasty.
1755 Massive earthquake destroys Lisbon and many other southern towns.

1807 Napoleon invades Portugal but is repulsed five years later.
1832–34 War of the Two Brothers resulting in a new and more liberal constitution.
1908 Republicans assassinate Carlos I in Lisbon.
1910 Birth of the republic.
1932–68 Salazar dictatorship.
1974 The Carnation Revolution, the drafting of a new democratic constitution and freedom for African colonies.
1986 Portugal joins the European Community.

Right: *Blue and white azulejos, often depicting historical scenes, are the most traditional form.*

Christian Reconquest and the Birth of a Nation

During the long years of Moorish occupation, northern Portugal had remained a lawless frontier area, and by the 11th century AD the county of **Portucale**, situated between the Minho and Douro rivers, had been regained for Christianity by the northern Spanish kingdom of Asturias-Léon. **Coimbra** followed soon after that. Northern Portugal came close to being absorbed by the emerging power of Léon-Castile but by 1179 **Afonso Henriques'** claim to be king of Portucale was recognized by the Pope, following victories against the Moors near his capital, **Guimarães**, and in Lisbon and Santarém. **Lisbon** was conquered with the aid of Crusader armies passing through en route to the Holy Land and, by the time of Afonso's death in 1185, Portugal's Christian frontier was the Tagus.

Afonso's son, **Sancho**, captured Silves, again with the aid of Crusaders, in 1189 but in 1190 a new and aggressive Moorish dynasty, the **Almohads**, once again advanced to the Tagus. By the middle of the 13th century the **Alentejo** and **Algarve** (Faro was the last Moorish stronghold to fall) had been incorporated into the expanding kingdom and the capital moved to Lisbon. The Algarve's separate status is underlined by the titles of the early rulers, who styled themselves **King of Portugal and the Algarve**. As land was reconquered, territory was given to those able to defend it, enabling the Church, the Knights Templar and the nobles to gain enormous power.

Conflicts with Spain

The principal threat to the new kingdom was now the rising power of Spanish Castile, which was jealous of Portugal's success in recapturing the Algarve. The Spaniards did not oust the Moors from Andalucía until 1492. Afonso III's son, **Dom Dinis** (1279–1325), built no fewer than **50 fortresses** along the Spanish border to protect the kingdom; many of these can still be seen in the Alentejo. Known as the **Rei Lavrador**, the farmer king, he introduced agricultural reforms, stimulated foreign trade and built up the navy. His wife, Isabel, later canonized as St Elizabeth, was famous for her charitable good works and promotion of peace. On her death in 1336 war broke out and a settlement was not reached until the Portuguese helped Castile defeat the Muslims in Andalucía in 1340.

Portugal's small population of approximately 500,000 had been decimated by the **Black Death**, and for the rest of the century **Castile** harried its western neighbour, claiming the throne by strategic marriages as well as sporadic invasions. In 1385 the Portuguese, although outnumbered, won the decisive battle of **Aljubarrota** with the help of a band of English archers. The **Treaty of Windsor** the following year was to become a permanent alliance between England and Portugal. With peace finally concluded, Portugal was free to turn its attention further afield. And with Castile lurking to the east, the only directions were west and south. The map of the world would never be the same again.

Below: *Queen Isabel, the wife of Dom Dinis, was famous for her charitable deeds.*

CARAVELS

The Great Discoveries were only made possible by a revolutionary design of sailing ship. Earlier ships were clumsy, with one mast and a square rig. Inspired by both the cargo-carrying *caravelas* of the Douro River and Arab dhows, the caravels' triangular sails enabled them to sail into the wind. The caravel was a lightweight and manoeuvrable vessel around 20m (66ft) long with three masts. Later models added a topsail and square sail for running before the wind. Columbus' favourite ship was a caravel, the *Niña*.

Opposite: *Visitors admire a restored compass rose.*
Below: *This reconstruction of a caravel demonstrates the craft's fine lines and lightweight build.*

The Great Discoveries

The Portuguese mapped the world as we know it, and established a **trading empire** which encompassed parts of South America, Africa, India, East Asia and the Spice Islands. They were the first Europeans to cross the equator, round the Cape of Good Hope and reach India by sea. They 'discovered' **South America**, landed in **Australia** 200 years before Captain Cook, and were the first to trade with **China** and **Japan**. The Portuguese almost certainly landed in **North America** before Christopher Columbus. Mariners from the Atlantic islands of the **Azores** (only discovered in 1427) were fishing for cod in the Grand Banks off **Newfoundland** 40 years before Columbus's epic voyage in 1492. But many did not return, and sailors' tales of their discoveries passed into oral myth.

Henry the Navigator

The driving force behind the great voyages was Prince **Henry the Navigator** (1394–1460), who became governor of the Algarve, moved to **Lagos** and founded a school of navigation. He used his personal fortune to employ some of the top cartographers and most experienced captains in Europe, convinced that there was more to the known world than the lonely wastes of the Atlantic.

In 1419 one of Henry's ships returned to port with the exciting news of a small uninhabited island 643km (400 miles) to the southwest. This was **Porto Santo**; a year later its sister island, **Madeira**, was discovered. The fertile volcanic island was colonized by farmers from the Algarve and by convicts from Lisbon, shipping in vines from Crete, sugar cane, cattle, wheat and barley.

With Madeira as a springboard, Henry drove his ships ever southwards and by the middle of the century the western coast of **Africa** had been opened up for trade; caravels laden with gold, slaves and ivory returned to the port of Lagos, and the income derived from these journeys financed future ex-

peditions. **Bartholomeu Dias** rounded the **Cape of Good Hope** in 1488; **Vasco da Gama** landed in **India** ten years later, and **Brazil** was claimed for Portugal in 1500.

The Age of Empire

In the 16th century Portugal was the richest nation in the world, with colonies and trading posts established in Goa, Malacca, Ceylon, the Spice Islands, Macau and the Persian Gulf as well as Africa and Brazil. Gold, ivory, silk, spices and silver flooded into the country. But the vast wealth that flowed into Portugal accrued to the Crown, the Church and the aristocracy and was dissipated by them. The great flowering of ideas of the European Rennaisance had considerable influence in Portugal, especially in the fields of sculpture, architecture and the decoration of the *azulejo* tiles.

The death of the childless Sebastião on a Moroccan battlefield in 1578 gave Philip II of Spain the opportunity he had been waiting for to seize the Portuguese throne. Sixty years of **Spanish rule** gained Portugal the enmity of her oldest ally, England (the Spanish Armada sailed from Lisbon to attack England in 1588), and also that of the Dutch. Vital trading agreements were lost and the two former allies mobilized to chip away at Portugal's overseas possessions.

THE LOST KING

Dom Sebastião's doomed expedition against Muslim forces in 1578 was one of the craziest campaigns in the history of warfare. A young and indulged sovereign, he was driven by an obsession to exterminate the Moors and at the age of 21 set sail for Morocco with a fleet of 500 warships and a force of 23,000 men. Suffering from heat exhaustion, they were no match for the defenders and no more than a few hundred escaped. Sebastião perished and, as he left no heir, Portugal was promptly annexed by Spain. But many believed that Sebastião had not died and would come back to make Portugal great again. As late as the last century the tradition among the aristocracy of placing an empty throne in their hall to await his return continued.

Economic Revival, Earthquake and the Marquês de Pombal

In 1640 national pride was restored when a popular revolt deposed the Spanish governor and put the **Duke of Bragança** on the throne. The subsequent discovery of **gold** and **diamonds** in Brazil sparked off a mass emigration and helped Portugal rebuild its faltering economy. The **Great Earthquake** of 1755 threw the nation into crisis but allowed the king's chief minister, the **Marquês de Pombal**, to push through some much-needed reforms.

Pombal was one of Portugal's most dynamic figures. He introduced state schools, set up export companies to promote the tobacco, whaling, fishing and port industries, abolished slavery, attempted to end discrimination by colour and religion, and expelled the very powerful Jesuits. His methods included the torture and imprisonment of his many opponents and he ended his days in disgrace, but his liberal reforms survived him.

The 19th Century

Napoleon invaded Portugal in 1807 and the monarchy fled to Brazil. Under British leadership the French were forced to withdraw, and a group of army officers demanded a new and more liberal **constitution** which included universal male suffrage and a curtailment of church and aristocratic privileges. This resulted in the **War of the Two Brothers**, with Miguel leading a reactionary counter-movement against his elder brother, Pedro, the heir to the throne. The war ended with a partial victory for the liberal side, and the rest of the century witnessed constant struggle between the supporters of democratic reform and conservatives.

The Republic

Republicanism was in the air and in 1908 the king and his eldest son were **assassinated** in Lisbon, shortly followed by an **army coup** which ended the monarchy. Manuel II escaped by boat to Gibraltar and ended his

THE GREAT EARTHQUAKE

It's a date every Portuguese school child knows by heart, and mentioning it invokes a Doomsday shiver. On 1 November 1755, All Saints' Day, most people were at mass when the Great Earthquake, estimated at a massive 8.9 on the Richter scale, struck. The tremors were felt as far away as Scotland and Jamaica but the epicentre was Lisbon. Much of the city was flattened and almost every church in southern Portugal was destroyed, along with the worshippers inside. At least 60,000 people died in the worst earthquake ever re-corded in Europe. Lisbon lost many priceless buildings and works of art, and also its status as one of Europe's finest cities and ports. Landslides, tidal waves and fires also devastated the Algarve towns of Faro, Tavira and Lagos.

days in comfortable exile in London. A series of short-lived and ineffectual governments came and went and in 1926 a military coup ushered in what was to become notorious as western Europe's most enduring authoritarian regime.

From Dictatorship to Democracy

Initially appointed Finance Minister, former economics professor **António Salazar** became Prime Minister in 1932. He was to control Portugal until 1968 and, while he undoubtedly improved and modernized the economy, he did so at the expense of democracy. Political parties, unions and strikes were banned and the **Church** clawed its way back into virtual control of education, the legal system and society. A **dictator** in all but name, Salazar was a great friend of Spain's General Franco and admired Hitler, although Portugal remained neutral in World War II.

His successor, **Marcelo Caetano**, promised more democracy but continued to wage deeply unpopular **colonial wars** in Africa. Discontent in the army crystallized into hardline opposition. In 1974, in a bloodless **left-wing revolution**, the army took over and was joined by socialists and democrats of all persuasions amid a mood of euphoric liberation and rejoicing. The **colonies** were granted **independence** following a general election. Portugal was finally free from the whims of kings, despots, cardinals and dictators and the country's fortunes were at last in the hands of its people.

EAST TIMOR: PORTUGAL'S CONSCIENCE

It was in 1999 that the true horror of Indonesia's brutal vendetta against the people of East Timor was finally revealed to a worldwide audience. Portugal had been campaigning against the Indonesian presence for decades, but the efforts of Portuguese diplomats to lobby for self-determination in the European Union and United Nations had largely fallen on deaf ears. Indonesian forces invaded the territory in 1975 after Portugal had withdrawn its administration. With the Portuguese nation itself in turmoil in the aftermath of the revolution, Portugal was powerless to resist. As well as attempting to mobilize international opinion and aid, Portugal has provided homes and education for thousands of displaced Timorese refugees.

Opposite: *The Marquês de Pombal is one of Portugal's most dynamic and controversial figures. This massive statue overlooks Lisbon's Baixa area, which he rebuilt in grid form after the Great Earthquake.*
Left: *Castles and shields feature prominently on Portugal's national flag; this version has been in use since the monarchy was ousted in 1910.*

Voting Patterns

45% Socialists	7% Conservative Popular Party
29% Social Democrats	11% Other
8% Green/Communist Alliance	

GOVERNMENT AND ECONOMY

Portugal is a multiparty democracy with parliamentary deputies elected by proportional representation every four years. The centre-right PSD, or Social Democrats, whose policies were popular in the 1980s, were defeated in 1995 by the **Socialist party** led by Antonio Guterres. In 2002 the Social Democrats returned to power, but with a narrow majority. Weak and increasingly unpopular, the government was forced to call early elections. The current prime minister is José Socrates, the PS (Socialist) leader, who was elected in 2005. The former mayor of Lisbon, Anibal Cavaco Silva, the veteran PSD man who led the party in the 1980s, is the current president. There are three tiers of government below the national level: **regional**, **municipal** and **parish**.

Below: *Parliament convenes in Lisbon's imposing Palácio da Assembleia da República, built around the 17th-century convent of São Bento.*

Economy

Since joining the European Union in 1986, Portugal has been an enthusiastic member and the recipient of grants to modernize infrastructure and industry. The road system in particular has been extensively improved. But economic growth has stalled and Portugal is still one of the poorest members of the EU, with a growing wealth gap between rich and poor, and undistinguished records in both education and social welfare.

Clothing and shoe making are strong areas in the manufacturing sector; industries such as steel, car manufacture, light engineering and cement are concentrated in the north of the country. Agriculture is in trouble and fishing declining, while tourism and service sectors record modest progress. Portugal's main trading partners are Spain, Germany, France, the UK and Italy. Portugal's main **industries** are the production of wood

pulp, paper and cork, foot-wear and textiles, tourism, wine, fish canning, oil re-fining and chemicals. In the **agricultural sector,** crop yields are well below the EU norm because of a lack of investment and scant use of machines and fertilizers. It is often cheaper to import vegetables and wheat from Spain than to produce them locally. The country is the world's leading exporter of tomato paste and cork. The main crops are wheat, barley, maize, rice, grapes for wine, tomatoes and potatoes.

Above: *Fishermen go about their business, overlooked by the high-rises of Albufeira in the Algarve. Tourism is a growth industry here, unlike fishing.*

Forestry and **fishing** are important but most of the fish caught are for domestic consumption. **Tourism** is a growth industry, employing half a million people and netting the country $5 billion in earnings from the 11 million international visitors the country receives every year. The Algarve, with its year-round good climate, attractive beaches and vast range of accom-modation options, receives the lion's share of tourists. The emphasis in developing tourism has switched from building modern hotels and high-rise apartment blocks near a beach to promoting the less-visited interior of the country. Families can receive grants to renovate often-crumbling old manor houses in rural areas and give them a new lease of life as guesthouses.

Portugal's **heavy industry** is concentrated in two areas, which between them account for three-quarters of the country's production. Oil refining, cement and wood pulp processing, steelmaking, car manufacture and ship-building are among the key activities in the **Lisbon–Setúbal** region. The **Porto–Braga–Aveiro** triangle in the north produces textiles, wood products, electronics and cutlery. Spain, Germany, France, the UK and other EU countries are Portugal's main trading partners.

ECONOMY

- **Inflation:** 2.4 per cent
- **Growth rate:** 2 per cent
- **Per capita GDP:** $21,800
- **Labour force:** 5.5 million (services 64 per cent, industry 30 per cent, agriculture, 6 per cent).
- **Unemployment rate:** 8 per cent
- **Population growth rate:** 0.39 per cent
- **Fertility rate:** 1.47 children per woman
- **Life expectancy:** 78 years

THE PEOPLE

The Portuguese people have been shaped by successive waves of migrants and invaders. The **Celts** settled here among the original Neolithic farmers; Greeks, Phoenicians and Carthaginians visited the south in smaller numbers. The **Romans** left a more lasting mark during six centuries of residence and were succeeded by Germanic Visigoths and Swabians. Then followed five centuries of **Moorish** occupation and, after the Great Discoveries, cross-fertilization from **Brazil** and the African and Asian **colonies**.

Despite this disparate blend of races and cultures, the Portuguese are a remarkably **homogenous** nation and quite distinct from their Spanish neighbours – much more laid-back and less macho. The Spaniards regard the Portuguese as old-fashioned country cousins and deride them for being 'Anglo Saxon' in their attitudes. This boils down to eating dinner early, not shouting much and being reserved rather than flamboyant. In return the Portuguese have a deeply ambiguous attitude towards Spain. 'Only ill winds and bad marriages come from Spain', is how the medieval proverb goes. On the one hand the Portuguese have more in common culturally with Spain than with other European countries. On the other hand they fear loss of independence – not politically as 500 years ago, but in terms of the global financial market and control of shared natural resources such as rivers. Spaniards are widely regarded as overbearing and arrogant and their superior buying power is envied.

As far as overseas visitors are concerned, the Portuguese are almost invariably **polite**, **hospitable** and **good humoured**. You should be aware that while the Portuguese are anything but inward-looking and jingoistic, national pride is strong. There are slight **regional differences** – in the north people tend to be

THE THREE R'S

Education is a key issue for the government, which recently allotted one fifth of its budget to improving schools. In 1989, 21 per cent of the population was illiterate but the figure fell to 8 per cent by 1997. Rather than representing a triumph for educators, this decline is largely due to the death of older country women, many of whom did not receive a formal education during the Salazar dictatorship. Over a third of the adult population cannot read or write beyond the most basic level and Portugal has one of the least-educated workforces in Europe. A third of all children still leave school before their 15th birthday, and there are many underage workers toiling in the factories of Oporto and Braga.

more serious and reserved and in the south there is a Mediterranean attitude to time. If you need someone's help in getting a problem solved it's best to build in a little flexibility. Things will happen eventually but probably not right this minute. 'Braga prays, Oporto works, and Lisbon plays', is one old saying which illustrates regional differences.

One characteristic trait of the Portuguese which has no English equivalent is **saudade**. This is a mood of bittersweet sadness, a recollection (on a personal level) of lost love, and on a national level a nostalgia for a lost Golden Age when Portugal ruled the seas. Nowadays many aristocrats have appropriated *saudade* to express their yearning for the Good Old Days when they were in charge and the peasants were grateful.

Society has altered radically in the past quarter of a century, from a **near-feudal** arrangement of rich landowners and industrialists, serviced by peasants and badly paid factory workers, to a dynamic **modern** society. When you look at Lisbon and Oporto's sharp-suited yuppies, mobile phones at the ready, or marvel at the number of smart new cars on the road, you may assume that progress is universal. But the gap in earnings between rich and poor, which fell after the Carnation Revolution in 1974, is rising again.

Language

Portuguese is the **third** most widely spoken European language in the world, after English and Spanish. It is spoken by 200 million people in the world, in Angola, Mozambique, Guinea-Bissau, Cape Verde, São Tomé and Principe, East Timor and Macau, as well as Brazil. It is a **Latinate** language and if you already speak Italian, French or Spanish you should be able to understand at least some words. Most Portuguese understand Spanish perfectly

PRONUNCIATION

Portuguese pronunciation is far from easy. When the tilde accent (~) is placed over ao (as in São) it creates an ow sound with just a hint of an oo to follow. An m at the end of a word is sounded like a combination of m and n; bom (good) sounds almost like bong, but the g is just a faint whisper. The letter s at the end of a word or before a consonant is pronounced sh; x and z also make a sh sound. The letter c is soft before e and I, hard otherwise unless it has a cedilla attached. The combination nh sounds like the ny of canyon.

Opposite: *The typical Portuguese dark good looks are a product of centuries of interaction with traders, invaders and the colonies.*

Below: *Service industries are booming in Portugal and executives are never seen without their mobile phones.*

FESTIVAL CALENDAR

Portugal's traditional festivals are fun to attend – ask at the local tourist office for more details on these events
• **February:** Carnival celebrations everywhere in the week preceding Lent. The most extensive are in Nazaré (Estremadura), Loulé (Algarve) and Ovar (Beiras).
• **March/April:** Holy Week festivals in Braga and Loulé (Easter Sunday).
• **May:** First of two annual pilgrimages to Fátima; Festa das Cruzes involves folk dancing and local crafts.
• **June:** Santarém's annual agricultural fair, held in the first week, includes bullfights, folk dancing and singing. Lisbon's St Anthony festival (12/13 June) has fireworks and bonfires all night. St John's Day (23/24 June) is a midsummer fire festival celebrated throughout the country.
• **August:** Festival in honour of Our Lady of Sorrow in Viana do Castelo; St Barbara's festival (lots of folk dancing) is held in Miranda do Douro (both third week in August).
• **September:** Ponte de Lima fair, featuring market and folk dancing.
• **October:** National gastronomy and folklore fair, Nazaré.
• **November:** National Horse fair, held in the first fortnight in Golegã (Ribatejo).

and, on paper at least, the two languages have many similarities. However, the characteristic **nasal sounds** and heavy inflection make spoken Portuguese difficult to understand. In tourist areas the vast majority of people you will come into contact with will speak English. If you need help and are looking for an English speaker, try a younger person as they are more likely to have learned English at school.

Religion

Portugal is overwhelmingly a **Catholic** country, with 97 per cent of the population at least nominally practising the faith. The north has always been more pious than the south, and the **Alentejo** in particular has a strong tradition of **anti-clericalism**. Regular churchgoing is very much confined to the **elderly**, apart from in the more traditionally minded north, and many churches are now permanently locked up for lack of custom. Nevertheless, **Romarias** (religious festivals in honour of patron saints) are widespread. Lisbon and many of the larger Algarve resorts have **Protestant** churches which provide services for visitors.

Right: *Portugal is becoming more secular but religious festivals, such as Festa dos Tabuleiros, are still popular.*

Sport

With 50 **golf courses** on the mainland, Portugal offers a huge choice for both holiday golfers and more proficient exponents of the sport. The greatest concentration can be found in and around **Lisbon** and the **Algarve**. Here the winter climate is ideal for golf and the area attracts thousands of enthusiasts from northern Europe every season. **Tennis** is also a popular sport and, while the Algarve has the most dedicated tennis centres, clubs and courts attached to hotels can be found throughout the country.

Above: *This dressage-trained Lusitano stallion is being put through his paces at Queluz Palace.*

Much of Portugal is excellent **riding** country and experienced riders will enjoy the thrill of handling the high-spirited (but generally well-behaved) **Lusitanos**, a native breed which is used for classical dressage displays. **Walkers** and **mountain bikers** too will find plenty of tracks and trails which will take them deep into the countryside. On the water, the Atlantic rollers provide world-class **surfing** at Guincho, north of Cascais, and indeed all along the western coast. **Windsurfing** is confined to sheltered estuaries such as Ferragudo in the Algarve, which is also home to sailing marinas such as Portimão and Vilamoura. Portimão is also the centre for **deep-sea fishing**. **Football** is a national obsession, with the most successful clubs based in Lisbon (Benfica and Sporting) and Oporto.

Bullfighting is still popular in southern Portugal despite protests from animal welfare groups. It is less unpleasant than the Spanish version, lacking the crowd's exultation in the kill, but you need a strong stomach to watch despite the marvellous horsemanship. The bull may not be killed in public, but will be slaughtered shortly after it leaves the arena exhausted and dripping with blood.

BULLFIGHTING

The Portuguese version differs in many respects from the better known Spanish spectacle. The bull is fought mainly from horseback and the *cavaleiro* plants *banderilhas* (barbed darts) into its neck muscles in a display of superb horsemanship and daring. Once the bull has been weakened it is wrestled to the ground by *forcados*, a team of athletic young men. In a variation, bulls are fought on foot in the Spanish style by a *toureiro* with a cape, but the death blow is symbolic. Killing the bull in the arena is illegal but the bull will be slaughtered after it leaves the arena exhausted and badly wounded. Most bulls for the arena are reared in the Ribatejo grasslands.

Above: *Portugal's unique Manueline architecture.*
Above right: *There is a strong artistic tradition in Portugal, ranging from abstract modern forms to traditional craftsmen, such as this street artist in Lisbon.*

MANUEL THE FORTUNATE

The reign of Manuel I (1495–1521) was Portugal's Golden Age. Known as Manuel 'the Fortunate', his assumed title was 'Lord of the Conquest, Navigation and Commerce of India, Ethiopia, Arabia and Persia'. He even dreamed of taking over Spain and to that end married the eldest daughter of Ferdinand and Isabella, the 'Catholic Kings' whose dynastic marriage had united the crowns of Aragon and Castile. But Manuel's dream was a delusion; Spain was poised to pounce on Portugal once again.

Architecture

Solidly built medieval castles and churches were virtually the only ancient buildings to survive the Great Earthquake of 1755. Look out for the **Romanesque** style of churches built in the 12th century after the Reconquest of Portugal, their strong and functional lines mirroring the fortresses of the period. The **Gothic** style, with its characteristic buttresses and pointed arches, was in vogue during the 13th and 14th centuries. During the 15th and 16th centuries Portugal developed its own unique architectural style, called **Manueline** after **Manuel the Fortunate**. The excitement of those heady times, when Portugal ruled the seas and dominated European trade, is reflected in the exuberant architecture. The shape remained basically Gothic but the style became much less formal and incorporated many exotic oriental touches. Columns and doorways were modelled into twisting ropes, and the **nautical theme** continued in knots, fishes, chains and anchors. Floral motifs and exotic animals were also worked into the extravagant designs.

From the mid-16th century onwards the classical symmetry of the **Renaissance** period took over, followed a century later by the excessively ornate **Baroque** interiors of churches and palaces, full of gold and gilded woodwork. The period of rebuilding after the Great Earthquake is dominated by simple **neo-classical** lines. Lisbon and Oporto both have some interesting **Art Nouveau** details. In the Algarve the **vernacular architecture** features many Moorish touches – filigree chimneys, arched windows, red tiled roofs, shady courtyards and latticework balconies.

Decorative Arts

Before the Romantic era of the 19th century most paintings concentrated on **religious themes** or **portraits** of wealthy patrons. Portuguese painters were greatly influenced by French, Italian and Flemish styles. Portugal has a strong tradition of **modern art**, with Paula Rego perhaps the most famous living artist. Contemporary **design** is equally strong and features uncluttered lines and vibrant colours. **Glazed tiles** (*azulejos*) are outstanding and designs range from traditional to modern.

Music and Performing Arts

Portuguese *saudade* reaches its fullest expression in *fado* music, Europe's own version of the blues. The name means 'fate' and the performers sing hauntingly of lost love and broken dreams to a guitar accompaniment. It is an emotional experience rather than entertainment and the audience is held spellbound. **Lisbon** and **Coimbra** are the two traditional centres of *fado*.

You'll hear the infectious rhythms of **African** and **Brazilian** music throughout Portugal, and Lisbon supports a number of **jazz** clubs. There are several active young **classical** composers, and both Lisbon and Oporto support **symphony orchestras** and **ballet** companies.

Folk music and **dancing** are associated mainly with country festivals, with Trás-os-Montes in the north home to several ancient and traditional forms.

DEATH OF A DIVA

Portugal's general elections in 1999 were overshadowed by the death of the Queen of *Fado*, Amália Rodrigues. She is one of only three internationally known Portuguese names – the other two being the footballer Eusebio and the dictator Salazar. Born in 1920 in the slums of Lisbon, Amália's matchless voice and sultry beauty aided her transition from dockside bars through professional *fado* houses to performances for visiting royalty and heads of state. She starred in a dozen films and made many of her finest recordings in the Sixties. Her emotional performances, extravagant style and refusal to bow to public opinion made her a superstar; prime minister Guterres spoke for many when he said at her funeral that she was 'the voice of the Portuguese soul'.

Below: Traditional folk dancers are still very much part of the local scene, particularly in the north.

Food

Eating well is one of the great pleasures of a holiday in Portugal. The food may not be particularly sophisticated (although there are plenty of smart restaurants in Lisbon, Oporto and the Algarve which offer the full fine dining experience) but it is invariably wholesome and home-grown.

Portugal's Atlantic coastline has endowed it with possibly the most extensive and freshest range of **fish** and **seafood** in Europe. It's often best plainly grilled; popular alternatives include *arroz de marisco* (seafood rice), *caldeirada* (fish stew) and *bacalhau à braz* (salt cod with scrambled eggs, potatoes and onions). In the Algarve, don't miss *amêijoas na cataplana*, a rich stew of clams, spicy sausage and ham served in a wok-like container.

If you're a meat eater, chicken, pork, lamb, kid and rabbit are generally better than beef. *Leitão assado* (roast suckling pig), *frango piri piri* (barbecued chicken in chilli sauce) and *carne de porco à alentejana* (pork with clams) are some of the highlights, as are *chouriço* (spicy sausage) and *presunto* (air-dried ham).

Everything comes with plainly boiled potatoes and **vegetables** in season or a simple salad – all of which are much more interesting than they sound as many vegetables are organically grown and locally produced and have that unique fresh-from-the-farm flavour. Locals complain that an increasing amount of vegetables are imported from Spain; these look good but taste bland. If you're self-catering, buy your vegetables from local markets rather than supermarkets. **Soups** are filling and the classic is *caldo verde*, made from potatoes and cabbage. **Fruits** in season include strawberries, cherries, grapes, melons, oranges, apples and delicious sweet

Left: *You'll need to dig deep into your pockets to purchase these venerable port vintages but there are plenty of affordable alternatives.*

Opposite: *Seafood fresh from the Atlantic and a chilled bottle of rosé: the perfect formula for an alfresco lunch.*

pineapples and bananas from Madeira. Local **cheeses** are well worth trying, particularly the soft ones made from ewes' or goats' milk, a speciality of the **Serra da Estrela** and **Serra da Arrábida** regions.

Portions are large (you can order a *meia dose,* or half portion) and you probably won't need a starter, particularly if you nibble at the bread, olives, fish pastes and bits of cheese which normally appear with the wine. Try and leave room for dessert; every region has its specialities but *pastel de nata* (custard tart), *queijada* (cheesecake), *pudim* (crème caramel) and *tarte de amêndoa* (almond cake) are among the tastiest.

Drink

The local **beers** (Sagres, Cristal and Super Bock) are refreshing lager-style brews. Portuguese **wine** is excellent and most of it is produced for local consumption so it is less well known on the international market than its quality warrants. House wine (*vinho de la casa*) is usually palatable and astoundingly cheap. Light white *vinho verde* is a refreshing summer drink and goes well with fish at lunchtime. Heavier meals call for reds such the burgundy-type **Dão** or the **Alentejo** vintages – those from **Reguengos** are among the best. After dinner enjoy a sweet **Madeira** or **Moscatel**, a glass of vintage **port** or *aguardente velha* – Portuguese brandy.

WINE LIST

Portuguese wines are not well known outside their own borders but they are as good as anything in Europe – and that, of course means very good indeed. Try the local wine wherever you happen to be – the only exception is the Algarve, whose home-grown efforts are very ordinary. If you like a big Burgundy-style red, try a Dão from the Beiras or a Reguengos from the Alentejo. Lighter reds include those from the Douro, a Torres Vedras from Ribatejo, and an Arruda or Colares from Estremadura. Light semi-sparkling *vinho verde* is fun in summer, but other northern whites are more serious – try one from the Ponte de Lima area. Arruda and Bucelas in Estremadura also produce flavoursome whites.

2
Lisbon

Lisbon is the most **southerly** European capital apart from Athens, and **warm weather** is one of its great assets. Even in January the sun shines with intensity; life is lived on the **streets** year-round, barring one of the downpours which occasionally punctuate the winter months.

Given the name **Alis Ubbo** (serene harbour) by the Phoenicians, Lisbon has been a Roman port, a Moorish fortress town, the richest city in Christendom, the epicentre of the most severe earthquake ever recorded in Europe, and now, in its most recent incarnation, a curiously **old-fashioned** city which is nevertheless modernizing fast.

Lisbon has a wealth of **historic sights** but one of its great idiosyncrasies is the way that not all is revealed on the first or even the fifteenth visit. Regular visitors are always finding new and fascinating corners of the city. There are over **40 museums** to discover and a top-class programme of classical **concerts** and **ballet** performances; or check out the vibrant late-night **club scene**, centred around the **Doca de Alcantara** and **Doca de Amaro**, which starts at 23:00 and continues until dawn.

But Lisbon is really about the pleasures of drinking **coffee** with a view of the ever-enchanting **Tagus**, which the Portuguese call the 'sea of straw' when it reflects the golden afternoon light. Or perhaps enjoying a good meal with excellent local wines at reasonable prices. Or the simple delight of wandering the jumble of streets which cascade up and down Lisbon's **seven hills**. It's very much a walker's city, although if you get footsore, hop on one of the famous antique **trams** – an experience in itself.

DON'T MISS

*** Belém: spend a whole day by the Tagus sampling an outstanding number and variety of cultural attractions.
*** Museums and galleries: Lisbon has lots, but if time is tight, visit the Museu Nacional de Arte Antigua, Museu Gulbenkian and Museu Nacional do Azulejo.
*** Alfama: stroll around this atmospheric old neighbourhood beneath the castle and enjoy the views.
** Nightlife: from *fado* restaurants to late-night club sounds, Lisbon has lots to offer.

Opposite: *The Torre de Belém is the unofficial symbol of Lisbon.*

Opposite: *Poet and writer Fernando Pessoa was a regular visitor to Café Brasiliera, which is still a meeting place for Lisbon's intellectual set.*

CITY CENTRE

By far the best way to explore Lisbon is on foot. Start at the **Rossio** in the heart of the Baixa, or lower town. Heading south, take the **Elevador de Santa Justa**, a wrought-iron lift dating from 1902. Pause to enjoy panoramic views of the city from the viewing terrace and then head west for the **Chiado** and the **Bairro Alto** before finishing at the **Praça do Comércio**. En route, stop for a coffee in the Art Deco surroundings of **A Brasileira** in Rua Garrett, which is still a favoured meeting place for Lisbon's intellectuals.

Rossio Square ★★

This is an unmistakable landmark – big, bustling and dominated by an equestrian statue of Dom Pedro IV and views of the **Castelo de São Jorge**. Shops and cafés line three sides of the square; on the northern side is the **Teatro Nacional de Dona Maria II**, built in 1846 on the site of a palace where the Inquisition plied its grisly trade. The typical mosaic pavements seen here are hand-cut white limestone and grey basalt cubes. Just to the east of the Rossio is another lively square, the **Praça da Figueira**, with an equestrian statue of Dom João I in the centre.

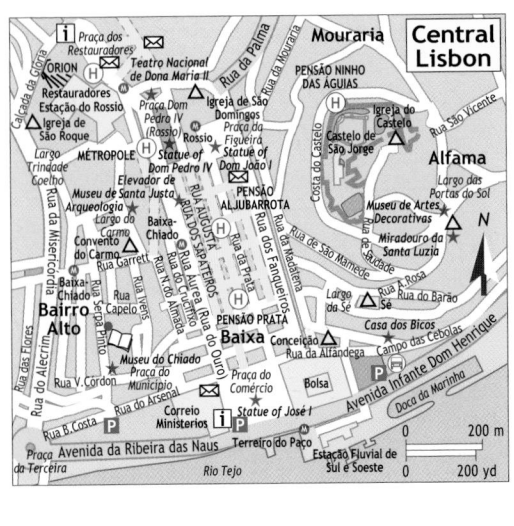

Igreja de São Roque ★★

Behind the plain façade, this small church, in **Largo Trindade Coelho**, is ornamented with some of the most expensive materials available – gold, agate, Carrara marble, alabaster, lapis lazuli and amethyst. The **chapel** left of the altar, Capela de São João Baptista, was designed and built in Rome in the mid-18th century and shipped to Portugal by royal command for a small fortune.

Bairro Alto ★★

The Bairro Alto is a **working-class** residential area with a growing number of trendy fashion boutiques, *fado* houses, bars and restaurants. There is a magnificent view over the Tagus from the **Miradouro do Alto de Santa Catarina** (Rua de Santa Catarina). The giant imprisoned in the rough-hewn statue is **Adamastor**, the Portuguese Poseidon who sailors believed would rise from the ocean depths off the African coast to wreck their flimsy caravels.

Chiado ★★

This smart shopping area was devastated by a fire in 1988 and is slowly being rebuilt. Memories of an earlier disaster are evoked by the ruins of the **Convento do Carmo** in Largo do Carmo; only the Gothic arches and walls remain of what was once one of Lisbon's largest churches, flattened in the 1755 earthquake.

The **Museu do Chiado**, at Rua Serpa Pinto 4, has a collection of a century's worth of Portuguese painting, which covers the period from 1850–1950. Open 10:00–18:00, closed Monday and Tuesday morning. Head east along the Rua do Arsenal, which was once one of the centres of the salt cod trade, to **Praça do Município**. On the east side is Lisbon's town hall, on the southern side the former arsenal, and in the centre a fine example of an 18th-century pillory. Continue until you reach the unmistakable Praça do Comércio.

Praça do Comércio ★★★

This vast open space was, until the earthquake destroyed it, the focal point of the city, dominated by a royal palace. Built to impress visitors arriving by sea, the square is one of the finest examples of the **Pombaline** style, named after the Marquês de Pombal who masterminded the rebuilding of Lisbon after the earthquake. The arcaded 18th-century buildings house

various government departments. The equestrian **statue** is of José I; behind it is a 19th-century Baroque **triumphal arch** decorated with allegorical representations of the great rivers of Portugal. Dom Carlos and his son were assassinated next to the post office in 1908.

Leaving the square at the seaward end, walk past the **Estação Fluvial de Sul e Soeste**, decorated with *azulejo* panels of towns in the Algarve and Alentejo. Passengers embark from here on ferries which connect with the train station for points south on the opposite bank of the Tagus. Turn left into Campo das Cebolas and admire the distinctive pyramid façade of the **Casa dos Bicos**, an early example of a rich man's folly which dates from the 16th century. Returning towards the Praça do Comércio, along the Rua da Alfandega, you will see the fine Manueline façade of the **Igreja da Conceição Velha**, rebuilt after the earthquake.

Between the Rossio and the Praça do Comércio is a grid of streets named after craftsmen's guilds which used to ply their trade here: **Rua dos Coreeiros** (saddlers), **Rua dos Sapateiros** (cobblers), **Rua do Ouro** (goldsmiths), and **Rua da Prata** (silversmiths). They are still full of old-fashioned specialist shops and there are plenty of cafés in the pedestrianized **Rua Augusta**.

THE ALFAMA

Sprawling down the steep hill between the castle and the **Tagus**, this is both the oldest district of Lisbon and in many ways the most authentic. It was inhabited by the Visigoths but the Moors made it their own, and the maze of alleys, vertiginous stairways and crumbling ochre-coloured buildings lend a unique atmosphere. But it's far from being a touristy 'old town', being a gritty and lived-in working-class area.

Sé (Cathedral) ★

The plain **Romanesque** style of this 12th-century building on Largo da Sé hints at its origins as a fortress. The interior contains many later **Gothic** features and includes the 14th-century **tombs** of Lopo Fernandes Pacheco, a companion of King Afonso IV, and his wife. They are both sculpted with their appealing-looking dogs at their feet. Excavations in the **gardens** of the Gothic **cloisters** have revealed Phoenician, Roman and Moorish remains. Open 10:00–18:00.

Castelo São Jorge ★★

Around 3000 years ago Lisbon's first inhabitants settled on this site and the Romans fortified it in their turn. But many of the castle's existing **towers** and **walls** date from the Moorish occupation. Stroll around and admire the views and the resident peacocks. Open daily 09:00–21:00 (18:00 in winter). There's also a multimedia presentation of the city's history (daily 10:00–13:00 and 14:00–17:30).

Beneath the castle are two further lovely viewpoints: the **Miradouro Santa Luzia** and **Largo das Portas do Sol** ('sun gateway'), one of the original seven gateways into the Moorish city. Between the two is the **Museu de Artes Decorativas** (open 10:00–17:00, closed Sunday), which contains a large collection of antique textiles, furniture, azulejos, paintings and porcelain.

BELÉM

To the west of Lisbon city centre is the district of Belém, the Portuguese word for Bethlehem. Here the **Tagus estuary** begins to open out into the Atlantic, and here in 1497 **Vasco da Gama** prayed all night in an old seaman's **chapel** for a safe return from his epic voyage to discover the sea route to India. After his triumphant return, Manuel I ordered the chapel replaced by a more fitting memorial, and in its place rose the stunning Mosteiro dos Jerónimos.

> **TRAMS**
>
> Almost a century old, these clanking old workhorses are a great way to get from A to B. They don't go fast so there's plenty of time to watch the world go by and spot interesting little corners you may care to revisit. Two of the most useful lines are the No 28, which runs from Estrela to Graça, passing through the Chiado and Baixa and trundling up and around the steep hills of the Alfama, and the No 15 which runs from Praça da Figueira and Praça do Comércio via Alcântara to Belém.

Opposite: *This imposing statue of José I, which dominates the Praça do Comércio, gazes out across the Tagus.*
Below: *Sightseers stroll along the medieval ramparts of the Castelo de São Jorge.*

Jardim do
Ultramar

Mosteiro dos
Jerónimos

Palácio
Nacional
de Belém

Museu de
Marinha

Museu

Centro
Cultural de
Belém

Nacional de
Arqueologia

Museu
Nacional dos
Coches

Av. da India

Museu de
Arte Popular

Padrão dos
Descobrimentos
(Monument of the
Discoveries)

Torre de Belém

Rio Tejo (Tagus River)

Av. da Torre de Belém

Opposite: *The Torre de
Belém is a magnificent
example of Manueline style.*
Right: *The Jerónimos
Monastery is an outstanding
historical site in Portugal.*

Mosteiro dos Jerónimos ★★★

This example of **Manueline** architecture was classified
as a UNESCO World Heritage Site in 1983. Built during
the 16th century and designed by Spanish, French and
Portuguese architects, the eclectic styles vary from
Gothic to **neoclassical.** The **south door** of the **Igreja
Santa Maria** is a riot of secular and spiritual carvings
and motifs. The sparse and graceful **interior** comes as a
surprise, with the huge octagonal **columns** seething
with vines and other vegetation. The **tombs** of Vasco da
Gama, Manuel I and another hero of the Portuguese
nation, the 16th-century poet **Luís de Camões**, are here.
The **cloisters** are beautiful; arrive early, before the
coach-borne crowds, to savour their peace. The
columns and walls are decorated with the Manueline
motifs of exotic birds and plants. Open 10:00–18:30.

The west wing houses the **Museu Nacional de
Arqueologia**. This has exhibits of **Bronze-Age** and
Roman jewellery and ceramics, coins and other
remains from Neolithic times through to the Moorish
period. Most impressive are the monolithic granite **boar
statues** from the north. Open 10:00–18:00, closed
Monday and Tuesday morning. Next door is the **Museu
de Marinha** which contains model ships, charts, navi-
gational instruments and paintings documenting
Portugal's **maritime heritage.** The full-size ceremonial
barges are impressive. Also on display is the original
seaplane which made the first crossing of the South
Atlantic in 1922. Open 10:00–18:00, closed Monday.

Museu dos Coches ★★

Founded in 1905 by Queen Amélia, the museum is located in the former **royal riding school** next door to the President's palace. This museum documents the pomp and ostentation of generations of Portuguese royalty through their ceremonial vehicles. Coaches, berlins, chaises, cabriolets, litters and sedan chairs from the 17th–19th centuries are on display here in all their velvet, brocade and gold Baroque finery. The most awesome are the 18th-century **Baroque coaches** designed for the Portuguese ambassadors to the Vatican. The Pope was no doubt impressed by these triumphal coaches incorporating full-scale sculptural friezes of heraldic beasts, gods, goddesses, heroes and infidels. Open 10:00–17:30, closed Monday.

Between the monastery and the sea is the bunker-like structure of the **Centro Cultural de Belém**, which may look decidedly unappealing but which hosts regular free concerts ranging from African and jazz to Portuguese pop and classical recitals in the Terrace Bar several evenings a week. During the day you can see touring art exhibitions, generally with a modern flavour. The new **Design Museum** (open daily, 11:00–20:00) documents modern style in three sections – pop, luxury and cool. Just opposite is the **Museu de Arte Popular** (open 10:00–12:30 and 14:00–17:00, closed Monday) which contains quirky exhibits of Portugal's **folk art** tradition – naive paintings, spiked dog collars, work tools, musical instruments and more.

Torre de Belém ★★★

This outstanding monument has become the unofficial symbol of Lisbon. It once stood on a rock in the middle of the estuary but because the course of the Tagus was altered after the Great Earthquake it is now close to shore. It was built in 1515 to act as a **lighthouse** and defend both the estuary and the Jerónimos Monastery. The stand jutting out from the base was a platform for

LISBOA CARD

If you want to pack the maximum sightseeing into your stay, buying this card should be a priority. It will give you free travel on almost all city transport and free entry into most museums and monuments. You will also get discounts on bus, tram and river tours. It's available in one-day, two-day and three-day versions and you generally recoup the reasonable cost of the card within a couple of hours. A discounted card for children aged from five to eleven can also be bought. It's available at several of the main attractions but the best place to buy it is at the Turismo de Lisboa offices at Rua Jardim do Regedor 50, opposite the Rossio train station, where you can also pick up free literature and guides to what's on.

Above: *The Discoveries Monument is a modern tribute to the explorers who mapped the world.*

artillery. Encircled by the crosses of the Order of Christ and embellished with Manueline twisting ropes, the tower displays plenty of influences from Venetian loggias to Moorish domes. The statue of the Virgin represents Our Lady of Safe Voyages.

Padrão dos Descobrimentos (Discoveries Monument) ★★

This striking sculpture, opposite the Jerónimos Monastery and looking proudly out to sea, was erected in 1960 to commemorate the 500th anniversary of the death of **Henry the Navigator**. He is at the prow and behind him are the explorers Vasco da Gama, Diego Cão and Ferdinand Magellan; other figures include Manuel I and Luis de Camões. Inside is an exhibition documenting the deeds of the discoverers and there's a fine view of both the Tagus and the monastery from the top. Open 09:30–18:30, closed Monday.

The final stop is not a monument but a shrine to good living – the **Pastéis de Belém** café (Rua de Belém 84). This café is one of the very best places in town to try Lisbon's traditional custard tarts, called *pastel de nata*.

ALONG THE TAGUS: FROM BELÉM TO PRAÇA DO COMÉRCIO

The **Ponte 25 de Abril**, named after the 1974 revolution, is Europe's second longest suspension bridge at 1013m (1108yd), spanning the River Tagus. If you're arriving from the south, the view of Lisbon from the bridge is impressive. The gigantic figure of **Christ** on the southern shore (28m/92ft high) is modelled on the statue of Christ the Redeemer in Rio de Janeiro and was erected in 1959 as thanks to the Almighty for having spared Portugal during World War II.

Just beneath the bridge is the **Doca de Santo Amaro**, formerly a run-down warehouse area but now an exciting late-night zone and full of bars, restaurants and clubs. It's also pleasant in the day for alfresco lunches overlooking the water. The **Doca de Alcantara**, just east, offers more of the same but is more slanted towards late-night action.

Museu Nacional de Arte Antigua ★★★

Housed in a 17th-century mansion at Rua das Janelas Verdes 9, this museum has an outstanding collection of religious art. The most famous Portuguese work is by the 15th-century master, Nuno Gonçalves. The theme is the adoration of St Vincent, the patron saint of Portugal, and the figures in the painting range from historical figures such as Henry the Navigator and Queen Isabella of Aragon to generic studies of fishermen, monks and Moorish knights. The other big attraction is the lurid *Temptation of St Anthony* by Hieronymus Bosch. One of the rooms contains ancient Japanese screens depicting the arrival of the Portuguese in 1543, and there is also a rich collection of gold and silver plate. Open 10:00–18:00, closed Monday and Tuesday morning.

THE ART OF COFFEE

Sipping coffee in a café is popular among the Portuguese. They also meet their friends here rather than at home. If you just ask for a *café* you will get a very strong espresso. Confusingly, if you want to order a small strong shot it may be best to specify *uma bica,* as some waiters are convinced that foreigners can't handle the real thing. But there are plenty of variations.

Bica cheia: espresso with extra water

Bica dupla: a double

Bica pingada: with a drop of milk

Um café com leite: coffee with milk

Um galão: hot milk with a dash of coffee

Café gelado: iced coffee

Um descafinado: a decaff (not that common in Portugal).

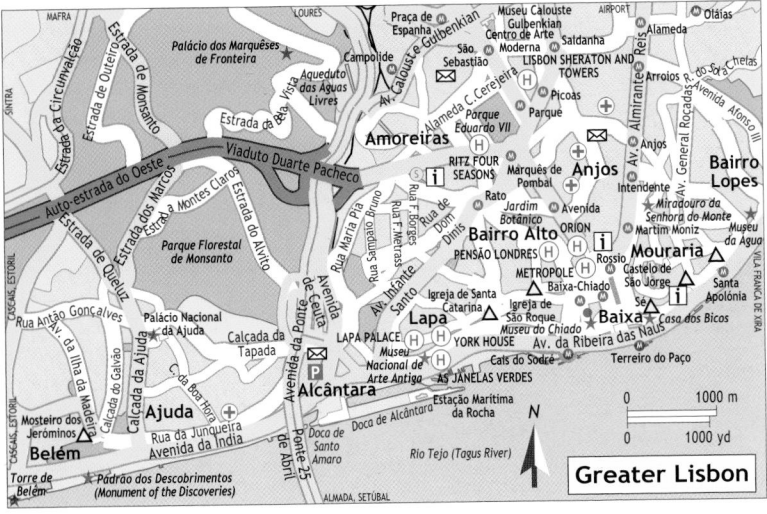

Greater Lisbon

BACALHAU

Bacalhau (salt cod) has been a staple of the Portuguese diet for 500 years, since fishermen roamed to the Grand Banks off Newfoundland and preserved their catch for the long voyage home. In the pre-fridge era it was easy to store at home. The tastiest variations of preparing *bacalhau* involve oven cooking with other ingredients.Try *bacalhau à brás*, where the fish is flaked into a savoury mix of potatoes, eggs, onions and olives; *bacalhau à nata* (oven-cooked in a cream and cheese sauce); *bacalhau deliciosa* (with prawns and cream); or *bacalhau con espinafre* (with spinach).

Below: *One of the many lovely tiles in the Museu Nacional do Azulejo.*

ALONG THE TAGUS: FROM PRAÇA DO COMÉRCIO TO EXPO

The riverfront area here is at present still under development but it does contain two interesting, if rather isolated museums, situated to the northeast of **Santa Apolonia** station. Take bus No 104 from Praça do Comércio or No 105 from Praça da Figueira.

Museu da Água ★

The Water Museum, at Rua do Alviela 12, demonstrates how Lisbon has coped with its chronic water shortage problems from Roman times onwards. Located in a former **water pumping station**, the museum contains four huge century-old **steam engines** and documents the engineering feat of Lisbon's 18th-century **aqueduct**. Open 10:00–17:00, closed Sunday.

Museu Nacional do Azulejo ★★

This is genuinely charming and the favourite museum in Lisbon for many. Set in a former convent at Rua da Madre de Deus 4, the National Azulejos Museum depicts the history and artistry of Portuguese *azulejos* from as early as the 15th century until the present day, with changing exhibitions featuring top contemporary artists. Among several highlights is a huge **panel** depicting Lisbon before the earthquake of 1755. The pleasant restaurant-café in an *azulejo*-filled patio is a good choice for a light lunch or a snack. Open 10:00–18:00, closed Monday and Tuesday morning.

Park of Nations ★★

Lisbon hosted **Expo** in the summer of 1998 and a lasting legacy was the development of a brand new urban regeneration site in the run-down docklands area. The best way to get there is on the Metro; the station opens into an

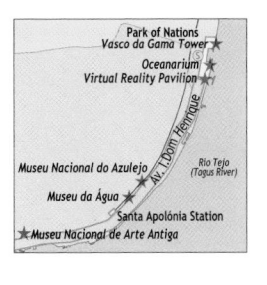

Left: *A visit to the Lisbon Oceanarium is enjoyable and informative.*

attractive new **shopping mall**. In the heat of summer, many families come here to stroll around, picnic and feel the fresh breezes blowing in off the Tagus. It's an equally good wet-weather attraction, with plenty of restaurants dotted around.

For a bird's-eye view of the site, take the lift to the top of the **Vasco da Gama Tower** or enjoy a cable car ride with views of Lisbon's newest **bridge**, an engineering feat spanning 18km (11 miles) which speeds traffic southwards and avoids the city. Regular **concerts** are held in the stadium and touring **exhibitions** in the remaining pavilions.

The top attraction is definitely the **Lisbon Oceanarium** (open daily, 10:00–19:00), the largest aquarium in Europe. The various aquariums represent the Atlantic, Pacific, Indian Ocean and Antarctic ecosystems, and touch-button technology illuminates interesting displays of ocean currents, whale migrations and prevailing winds. Each habitat is full of representative sea creatures and vegetation, from puffins, rays and sharks to corals. Everyone's favourite is the family of sea otters, which roll and play in a big landscaped tank and crunch prawns while lying on their backs. **The Virtual Reality Pavilion** (open 13:00–19:00, closed Monday) provides an imaginative tour of the ocean floor complete with sounds and smells as well as sights.

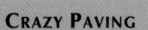

CRAZY PAVING

Look down as you roam the streets and spot some of the exotic patterns which swirl across the pavement – caravels, shields, waves, stars, animals, birds and anchors are just some of the motifs. Lisboan pavements have been hand-built by artisans for over a century and a half, a tradition which survives today. Many of the pavements in the **Parque des Nações** have been handcrafted although the design was conceived on computer. The **Rossio** was the first square to be paved with black and white stones in 1842; five years later every central square was covered in mosaics. Each stone is hammered by hand and the ground prepared by digging a box to the depth of 8cm (3in), which is then covered with a mixture of sand and rubble. After placing the stones in their pattern, more sand is added to fill in the gaps and the finished article is doused in water and hammered to set.

St Vincent may be the official patron saint of Lisbon but St Anthony, miracle worker and matchmaker, is the one they all love. And if you love a good party, June is the month to be in Lisbon. Liveliest night is 12 June, the eve of the feast of St Anthony, when traditional neighbourhoods such as Castelo, Alfama and Graça hold community street parties with barbecued sardines, lots of beer and wines, music and dancing. The feast of St John on 24 June is more an Oporto thing, but gypsies from all over the country converge on the **Parque Eduardo VII** for a traditional festival. The night of the 28th, the eve of St Peter's Day, is another occasion for street parties, with some communities still building bonfires in the streets in an echo of pre-Christian midsummer fertility rites.

NORTHERN LISBON

This is the modern part of the city and sights here are scattered but still worth a visit. Heading north up the impressive **Avenida da Liberdade**, you can't miss the enormous statue of the **Marquês de Pombal** with a lion in tow. Behind him the formal gardens of **Parque Eduardo VII**, with hothouses, cool houses and an ornamental lake, provide a pleasant view south to the Tagus. The **Jardim Botânico**, west of Avenida da Liberdade, has a lovely avenue of palm trees and many other sub-tropical plants; it's another nice spot for a stroll or perhaps a picnic when the temperature soars. From the northern suburbs you'll also get a glimpse of the mighty **aqueduct** spanning the Alcantara valley, a 941m (881yd) sequence of rounded and Gothic arches which was a masterpiece of hydraulic engineering in the 18th century.

Museu Gulbenkian and Centro de Arte Moderna ★★★

This excellent museum (Metro: São Sebastião) has an eclectic collection, with the main categories comprising **Oriental** (Egyptian, Roman, Persian, Chinese); **European** art of the 18th and 19th centuries, including works by Turner, Monet, Manet, Renoir and Degas; **Flemish** and **Dutch** masters, including Rembrandt and Rubens; and a room devoted to the **Art Nouveau** creations of the designer **René Lalique**, who was a personal friend of the museum's patron. The **Centro de Arte Moderna** next door holds the best collection of **contemporary Portuguese art** in the country; Maria Helena Vieira da Silva, Amadeo de Souza Cardosa, José de Almada Negreiros and Paula Rego are among those featured. Open 10:00–18:00, closed Monday and Tuesday mornings.

Palácio dos Marquêses de Fronteira ★★

Built as a **hunting lodge** in 1670, the architecture of this fine palace and gardens (Metro: Sete Rios) is influenced by the Italian Renaissance. The **gardens** are perhaps more interesting than the interior, with lots of Classical statuary, fountains and an ornamental lake. There are also gorgeous *azulejos* depicting nature and rustic themes. Open 10:30–12:00, closed Sunday.

Palácio Nacional de Queluz ★★★

Once a rural retreat for royalty and now incongruously set among the tower blocks which sprawl north from Lisbon's suburbs, this **Rococo gem**, which can be reached by rail from Rossio, is Versailles in miniature, complete with formal gardens. It was built in the mid-18th century and one wing of the palace is still used to accommodate visiting dignitaries.

The **Throne Room**, a symphony of crystal chandeliers, gold Baroque edgings and ornamental mirrors, was evidently designed to impress. The tour continues through the more mundane dining, smoking and coffee rooms to the lovely *Azulejo* **Room**, where floor-to-ceiling yellow and blue tiles represent rural scenes from Portugal's tropical colonies, plus neoclassical depictions of Portuguese gentry at play in their country estates. The **Ambassadors' Room**, with a fine chequered marble floor and a colourful painted ceiling, and **Pedro IV's bedroom**, enlivened by scenes from Don Quixote on the walls, are the other highlights. Outside in the formal grounds are Classical **statues**, a boating canal and fountains. There are occasional Classical **equestrian displays** in summer; check with the tourist office for times. The palace is open 09:30–17:30, closed Tuesday.

LUSITANO – MOUNT OF KINGS

The Portuguese Lusitano horse is a breed with a proud pedigree. The quality of these handsome horses was renowned throughout Europe in medieval times; its ancestors were the spirited Arab and Barb horses brought over by the Moors. The National Stud was founded in 1748. The Lusitano is an excellent lightweight riding horse, standing around 15.2 hands high, and is normally grey, brown or bay. Fast and intelligent, but with a friendly nature, they can be tried out in riding schools around the country. You can also see these magnificent horses take part in classical dressage displays at historic venues such as **Queluz Palace** near Lisbon.

Opposite: *The festival of St Anthony in June is Lisbon's carnival, complete with colourful processions.* **Left:** *The Throne Room in the Palácio Nacional de Queluz is a symbol of the opulence enjoyed by Portuguese monarchs.*

Lisbon at a Glance

Lisbon is a year-round city and can provide a sunny escape during the winter months but visitors should be prepared for rain – pack a raincoat and wear sensible shoes as the limestone pavements can get slippery. Frost is virtually unknown. The wettest months are **Nov** to **Mar. Apr, May** and **Sep** are normally beautiful months and are not too hot for sightseeing; temperatures can soar in **Jul** and **Aug** and you may want to spend the extra on a hotel with a pool – not a common commodity in Lisbon where space is at a premium.

Lisbon is the international gateway to Portugal and is also linked to **Faro** and **Oporto** by regular air services. There is a tourist office in the arrivals concourse of the airport. The airport is a 20–40 minute drive from the city centre depending on traffic. A handy airport bus runs down the Avenida da Liberdade, with a stop in Praça dos Restauradores near the tourist office, to Cais do Sodré station. It's free to **TAP Air Portugal** customers; just show your ticket. Otherwise there is a small charge in the form of a one- or three-day travel pass which you can then continue to use on other buses, metros and trams in the city. Taxis are reasonably priced but you should have your address, written in Portuguese, to hand.

Insist the meter is switched on.

You can get a transport map from the tourist office or from the Carris kiosks located in Praça da Figueira and at the bottom of the Elevador Santa Justa. Here you can buy one- or three-day Bilhete Turístico, passes valid for **buses, trams,** the **metro** and **funiculars**. If you are going to visit a lot of sights, the Lisboa Card, available from the tourist office, is a better bet as it includes admission to museums. You can pay for individual journeys on buses and trams and at metro stations. Public transport runs from 06:00 to 01:00. The metro is clean and efficient but crowded during rush hours. Look out for signs indicating Correspondência (transfer between lines) and Saída (exit to street level). Don't bother to hire a car while you're in the city – the traffic is chaotic and parking spaces are scarce. **Taxis** are cheap and plentiful and can be hailed at ranks in the main squares and stations. Radio Taxis de Lisboa, tel: 21 811 9000, is the largest radio taxi company. Unfortunately many taxi drivers are unscrupulous about taking tourists for a ride; have your address written down, try and follow your progress on the map and insist the meter is switched on. If you think you have been cheated, get a receipt, the driver's

official number and complain to the tourist police.

LUXURY
Lapa Palace, Rua do Pau da Bandeira 4, 1200 Lisbon, tel: 21 394 9494, www.lapa-palace.com Former mansion, now plush five-star with antiques, gardens and pool where celebs stay.
York House, Rua das Janelas Verdes 32, tel: 21 396 2435, www.yorkhouselisboa.com Once a 17th-century convent, now a top-class small hotel.

MID-RANGE
Residencial das Janelas Verdes, Rua das Janelas Verdes 47, tel: 21 321 8200, www.heritage.pt Small appealing former mansion with pretty patio.
Hotel Metropole, Praça do Rossio 30, tel: 21 321 9030, www.almeidahotels.com Right on Rossio Square, friendly three-star hotel with air conditioning.
VIP Eden, Praça dos Restauradores 24, tel: 21 321 6600, www.viphotels.com One-bedroom apartments and studios, 24-hour reception, rooftop pool, very central; the longer you stay, the more reasonable the rates.

BUDGET
Most of the accommodation in this sector is situated in the Baixa and Rossio area, and the city tourist office can help you find somewhere, although

they can't make bookings.

Pensão Aljubarrota, Rua da Assunção 53–4, tel/fax: 21 346 0112. Baixa B&B with Italian management and good views of the castle.

Pensão Ninho da Aguias, Costa do Castelo 74, tel: 21 885 4070. Just beneath castle, with good views and a pretty garden.

Pensão Londres, Rua Dom Pedro V 53, tel: 21 346 2203, www.pensaolondres.com At the top of the Elevador da Gloria, good value and very popular so book ahead.

WHERE TO EAT

There are hundreds if not thousands of restaurants in Lisbon. This small selection is located around the Rossio/Bairro Alto area.

Bica do Sapato, Cais da Pedra à Bica do Sapato, tel: 21 881 0320. Up-market warehouse conversion by the river, partly owned by John Malkovich.

Casa do Alentejo, Rua das Portas de Santo Antão 58, tel: 21 346 9231. Old building with lots of atmosphere, good regional cuisine from the Alentejo.

Cervejaria da Trindade, Rua Nova da Trindade 20C, tel: 21 342 3506. Wonderful 19th-century *azulejos*, big bustling mid-priced restaurant.

Pap'Açorda, Rua da Atalaia 57, tel: 21 346 4811. Excellent food, theatrical decor, popular with celebs.

Primavera, Good, honest Portuguese food in this long-established restaurant in the Bairro Alto. Josephine Baker, the 'Jazz Cleopatra', used to eat here. Travessa da Espera 34, tel: 21 342 0477.

A Comida da Ribeira, Mercado da Ribeira, tel: 210 312 600. Check out the market and then have lunch in this popular spot.

TOURS AND EXCURSIONS

Lisbon Walker (guided tours), tel: 218 861 840.

Cruzeiros no Tejo (for river cruises from Estação Fluvial), tel: 21 882 0348.

Carris (offers tram and open-top bus tours), tel: 21 361 3078.

Lisbon Welcome Centre, Rua do Arsenal 15, Praca do Comercio, tel: 210 312 810, www.visitlisboa.com

USEFUL CONTACTS

Portuguese Tourist Office (ICEP), Palácio Foz, Praça dos Restauradores, tel: 21 346 3314, www.visitportugal.com At either of these offices pick up **What's On in Lisbon**, a monthly English-language

guide to entertainment and events, plus sightseeing and transport tips.

Hospital Britânico, Rua Saraiva de Carvalho 49, tel: 21 395 5067 or 397 6329. English-speaking medical staff.

Tourist Police, Palacio Foz, Praça 20, Restaura dores, tel: 21 342 1634. For general emergencies dial **112**.

SAFETY

The city is generally safe but thieves and muggers do target tourists. If you have a car, never leave anything of value inside. When out, take a bag for your camera if you feel it is attracting unwelcome interest. Leave valuables, tickets and passports in the hotel safe or with reception, and only take what you need for the day. Never keep your wallet in an outside pocket or in your hip pocket; women should try and carry cash and cards on their person rather than in a handbag. At night, both men and women should avoid walking alone in the Alfama and Barrio Alto.

LISBON	J	F	M	A	M	J	J	A	S	O	N	D
AVERAGE TEMP. °C	11	12	14	16	17	20	22	23	21	18	14	12
AVERAGE TEMP. °F	51	53	57	60	63	69	72	73	71	65	58	52
HOURS OF SUN DAILY	5	6	6	8	9	11	10	11	8	7	5	5
RAINFALL mm	111	76	109	54	44	16	3	4	33	62	93	103
RAINFALL ins.	4.3	3	4.2	2	2.1	0.6	0.1	0.2	1.3	2.4	4	4.1
DAYS OF RAINFALL	15	12	14	10	10	5	2	2	6	9	13	15

3
Around Lisbon and Central Portugal

Lisbon's appeal doesn't end with the city limits. There are few other capital cities in Europe where you can enjoy such a range of diverse scenery and activities within a hour's easy journey of the centre. The sandy beaches, mini mountain ranges and beautiful woods of both the **Costa Azul** to the south and the **Estoril/Sintra** area to the north beckon. Here you can walk, ride, swim, play golf or head for the hills in a jeep safari. **Sintra** in particular has plenty of heavyweight cultural attractions which no visitor to Lisbon should miss. An increasing number of visitors opt to stay in Sintra itself or the nearby seaside resorts of **Estoril** and **Cascais** and commute to Lisbon for a day's sightseeing rather than the other way around.

Moving north, explore Portugal's rural heartland of the **Ribatejo** and **Beiras** and leave the crowds behind. The mighty **River Tagus** winds through flat plains where fine Lusitano horses are raised alongside bulls for the arena. Lovers of wild mountain scenery should be in their element in the **Serra da Estrela**, the Mountains of the Stars. If you enjoy **fine wines** and hearty **regional cuisine** you should sample the local vintages and dishes. You can visit the ancient city of **Coimbra**, the Oxford of Portugal, and see the Roman ruins of nearby **Conimbriga**.

To the west, the province of **Estremadura** has many architectural treasures, along with miles of largely uncrowded sandy beaches. The **coast** is a magnet both for surfers who can tackle the Atlantic rollers and those who prefer the less challenging pleasures of sunbathing and eating superb seafood in quiet seaside surroundings.

DON'T MISS

★★★ Sintra: moody and full of atmosphere, this romantic little town is definitely something special.
★★★ Batalha: while here, marvel at the flamboyant Gothic/Manueline architecture of the town's impressive monastery.
★★ Costa Azul: Portugal in miniature, with a mini mountain range and beautiful sandy beaches.
★★ Óbidos: Stroll around the castle walls and indulge your medieval fantasies.

Opposite: *The twin chimneys of Sintra's Palácio Nacional are its most striking feature.*

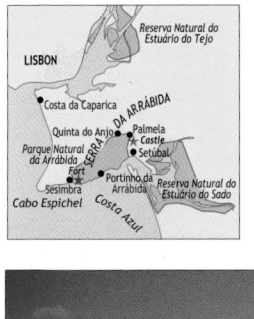

Costa Azul

The 'Blue Coast' is the tourism name for the Setúbal Peninsula on the south bank of the Tagus. It's a favourite spot for Lisboans to enjoy the seaside life on summer weekends. Most head for the **Costa da Caparica**, the closest stretch of beach to the capital, but the best coves are further away on the south coast. **Setúbal**, a commercial port, is the largest town, and is a good base if you want to sample some of the activities in the area. One unique excursion is dolphin-spotting in the **Sado Estuary**, which is home to a resident population of around 30 bottlenose dolphins. Look out too for flamingos, storks, marsh harriers and egrets in the mud banks, marshes, salt pans and lagoons which line the shores.

Serra da Arrábida ★★

This mini mountain range, extending for 35km (22 miles) from **Palmela** to **Cabo do Espichel**, is a natural park. A warm microclimate has resulted in a rich variety of Mediterranean vegetation, including aromatic herbs, wild flowers, olives, holm oaks, myrtle and mastic trees. Notable birds include Bonelli's eagle, buzzards, bee eaters, eagle owls and barn owls.

The **castle** at Palmela has been partially converted into a *pousada* (hotel) and gives lovely views westward over the hills. On a clear day you can see as far as Lisbon and the Serra da Sintra. Nearby, in **Quinta do Anjo**, visit the **Fortuna** ceramic workshop for a fascinating insight into this traditional art.

A scenic drive west along the coast from Setúbal will reveal the steep side of the Serra, with cliffs plunging down to the sea and beautiful scenery which recalls the French Riviera. **Portinho da Arrábida** is a lovely sheltered sandy beach which gets busy at weekends. Look out for the yellow house on the cliffs where Queen Elizabeth II stayed – she certainly had a view fit for a queen. The 16th-century **Convento da Arrábida** above is now a residential conference centre.

Above: *Sesimbra's Santiago Fort once guarded the entry to the Sado Estuary.*

Sesimbra ★

This is a very pleasant seaside resort which retains something of its original fishing village charm. It has a big **beach** and plenty of **watersports** in summer; fishermen land swordfish among the windsurfers. The **Santiago Fort** on the beach dates from the 17th century, and the ruined **castle** overlooking the town was built by the Moors.

Cabo Espichel ★

Further west is Cabo Espichel, where the Serra plunges into the sea. It's a wild and desolate spot. The 18th-century church of **Nossa Senhora do Cabo** here is the focus of an annual pilgrimage in September. Two local fishermen were in danger of being wrecked in a storm and a vision of the Virgin guided them to shore, or so the story goes. The ruined buildings are where the pilgrims lodged.

REGIONAL SPECIALITIES

Vines have been grown on the northern slopes of the **Serra da Arrábida** for centuries and, like **Colares** near Sintra, this was the only region in Portugal to escape the deadly phylloxera virus – it could not penetrate the sandy soil. As in Colares, the wines here are delicious and of ancient stock. Try the Moscatel, a sweet variety, unique to the region. Honey is also excellent as the bees feed on herbs and wild flowers, and the soft Azetão cheeses are exceptional.

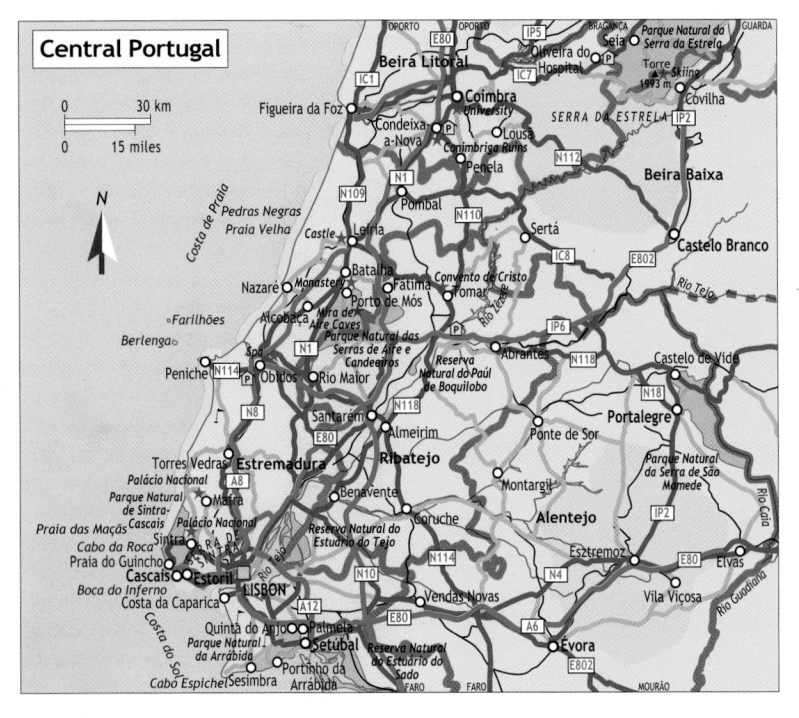

Central Portugal

THE HISTORY OF SINTRA

Sintra was a sacred spot for the Celts who called the area the Mountains of the Moon. In 1147, the Palácio Nacional became the summer retreat for the court. Two turning points in Portuguese history were planned here. In 1415, the conquest of Ceuta was ordered. In 1578 Dom Sebastião decided to invade Morocco. His defeat marked the end of the Golden Age and Spain took control of Portugal. In the 18th century Sintra became a haunt of the aristocracy, poets and artists from all over Europe and continues this reputation today.

SINTRA

There are few places in the world that combine art, beauty, nature and magic in quite such an enchanting way as Sintra. The town's coat of arms, with its tower, crescent moons and stars, is more tarot card than heraldic shield and it continues to weave its magic over modern visitors. The great **palaces,** misty **mountains**, mossy **gardens**, mysterious **woods**, and old **mansions** are impressive in their own right but the total effect is much greater than the sum of the parts.

Palácio Nacional de Sintra ★★

First fortified by the Moors, the site was converted into a **royal palace** in the 15th century and became a favourite retreat for generations of royalty. Irregular in structure, the architecture reflects centuries of add-ons. The most striking external feature are the huge twin **chimneys**. Highlights of the interior include the *azulejos* in the **Sala dos Árabes**, the heraldic shields of the **Sala das Armas** (Armoury Room) and the swan ceiling of the **Sala dos Cisnes**. Open daily 10:00–17:00, closed Wednesday.

Museu de Arte Moderna ★★

This relatively new art gallery, situated on Avenida Heliodoro Salagado, in the modern part of town, is a cheery antidote to the collections of gloomy religious art. The **surrealists** are here in force (Max Ernst, Joan Miró, Man Ray and René Magritte among them), **Jackson Pollock** is featured in the abstract

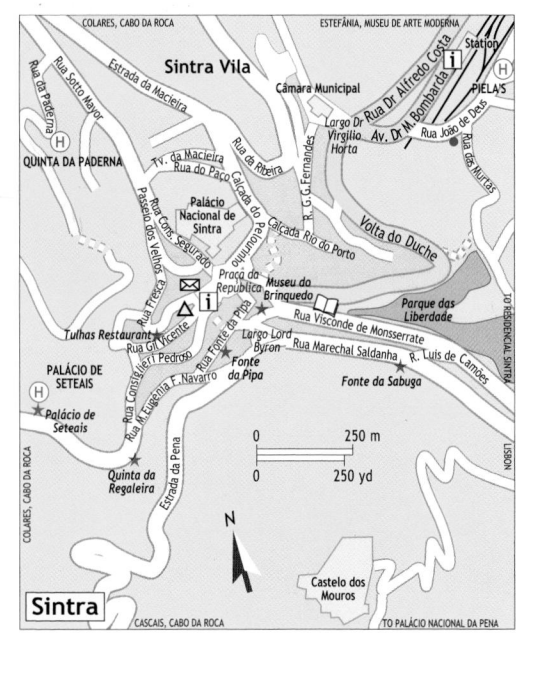

expressionist wing, and upstairs is an excellent collection of **pop art** including works by Andy Warhol, Roy Lichtenstein and Gilbert and George. Don't forget to check out the top floor café and restaurant, which offers an outdoor terrace and nice views. Open 10:00–18:00, closed Monday.

Quinta da Regaleira ★★★

This fairytale mansion was built a century ago in **mock-Manueline** style for a Portuguese millionaire, António Carvalho Monteiro, who had made his fortune in Brazil. A noted Freemason and occultist, Carvalho also created a magical **garden** where he and his friends could hold their rituals. The initiation well is a hollow **tower** descending into the hillside

through nine levels, entered by a secret revolving door. Throughout the gardens and woods are classical statues, stone altars, meditation lakes, grottos and fountains, with the stonework richly decorated in symbols. The interior of the *quinta* is a bit tame but the exterior is fabulous, literally dripping with Manueline features – strange fruits, ropes, nets, frogs and dragons among them. Open daily 10:00–18:00, reservations essential for tour, tel: 21 910 6650.

Above: *The sumptuous and mysterious magical gardens of Quinta da Regaleira retain plenty of atmosphere.*

Palácio de Seteais ★

This **neoclassical mansion**, now converted to a luxury **hotel**, was built in the 18th century for the Dutch consul. It was subsequently bought by the Marquês de Marialva, the most powerful nobleman in Portugal, whose rather decadent parties were documented by the English exile **William Beckford**. Guests at the mansion could expect over 35 courses at the banquets, with the entertainment provided by, among others, musicians, dwarfs, animal acts and even children dressed as angels. The formal **gardens** and **views** are stunning; to view the antique-filled interior, you will probably have to book a room at the hotel or at least have a meal.

> #### HOUSE OF THE SEVEN SIGHS
>
> Seteais means Seven Sighs in Portuguese and this is how the mansion got its name. A Portuguese nobleman fell in love with a Moorish princess who had escaped from the besieged citadel of Sintra. Unfortunately she was under a spell and could only say 'ai' seven times before she died. Her first 'ai' was when she first set eyes on her Portuguese lover. Four more 'ais' followed during their affair. When he left her to go to the wars she uttered her penultimate 'ai' – the last was when her Moorish ex-boyfriend killed her in revenge.

Palácio Nacional da Pena ★★★

It's a very steep 90-minute walk up to this **fantasy palace** and you may prefer to take the bus up with the option of walking down through the wooded park, which is lovely, with huge redwoods, beautiful exotic plants, lakes and follies.

This remarkable building was constructed in the 19th century by the Bavarian **Ferdinand Saxe-Coburg-Gotha**, the husband of Queen Maria II, with the help of a German architect, Baron Eschwege. It has a bit of everything: turrets, domes, tunnels, parapets, crenellated walls and a draw-bridge, and is painted in garish colours. Architecturally it's a mishmash of Gothic, Manueline, mock-Arab, Renaissance and Baroque – of everything, in fact, but good taste. The interior is just as the royal family left it in 1910, when they fled on the eve of revolution, and is full of **antique furniture**, rich drapes and paintings. Open 10:00–17:30, closed Monday.

Above: *Colourful and displaying an eclectic mix of architectural styles, the Palácio Nacional da Pena dominates the Sintra skyline.*
Opposite: *Atmospheric old quintas abound in the countryside; many now enjoy a new lease of life as small hotels.*

Serra da Sintra ★★★

Sintra's granite mountain range reaches its highest elevation of 529m (1736ft) at the **Cruz Alta** which overlooks the Pena Palace. Lord Byron called it a 'variegated maze of mount and glen'; it's rugged, often misty and rainy, and covered by romantic woods. Oaks, chestnuts, cedars, camellias, rhododendrons, ferns and moss flourish here among many other subtropical plants. Try to pick up a map of walking routes from the Natural Park's headquarters in Sintra. There are many atmospheric old **mansions** in the surrounding countryside where you can stay and savour the peace and beauty of the hills.

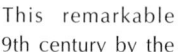

CASTELO DOS MOUROS

The path down to town from the Palácio Nacional da Pena passes by the Castelo dos Mouros (Moorish Castle) which was restored in the 19th century but is still basically a ruin. There are towers, a keep, a small Romanesque church and walls which snake along the precipices. The views over Sintra are marvellous.

AROUND SINTRA

If travelling by car, leave Sintra by the Pena Palace road and turn off towards Cabo da Roca. The first stop is **Convento dos Capuchos** (open daily 10:00–17:00). This tiny underground hermitage was built in 1560 to house a dozen Capuchin monks. Surrounded by a jumble of huge boulders and tall trees, the monks lived and prayed here in tiny cork-lined cells. At **Peninha** there's a small chapel with an *azulejo*-filled interior and panoramic views of **Praia do Guincho**, one of the top surfing beaches in Europe. The Serra da Sintra plunges into the sea at **Cabo da Roca**, a sheer cliff 140m (459ft) above the sea. This is continental Europe's most westerly point – wild, rugged and dramatic.

Return inland and rejoin the N247 heading north to **Colares**. This is the home of some of the finest wines in Portugal, the vines from ancient stock and grown on sandy soil which give their unique character. If it's a hot day you may want to detour to **Praia das Maçãs** for a swim. The **Monserrate Gardens** are 4km (2.5 miles) west of Sintra; covering 30ha (74 acres), they were created in the 18th century and enlarged with many tropical additions in the 19th. Wild and rambling rather than formal, they are a lovely spot for a walk or a picnic and are open daily 09:00–18:00.

Palácio Nacional de Mafra **

Half an hour's drive north of Sintra, this massive 18th-century palace is worth a visit. Built by Dom João V and financed by the Brazilian gold rush, the project at one time had 45,000 labourers working on site. Highlights include the pastel pink and blue Italianate basilica and the enormous library which contains 40,000 books. The dining room has gloomy candelabra composed of stags' antlers, and dozens of hunting trophies line the walls.

GOLF

The area around Sintra has no less than a dozen top-class courses. The championship course at Estoril is one of the oldest in Europe while the more recent Penha Longa course has hosted several Portuguese Opens. Other courses may not be quite as testing but still offer an enjoyable game in beautiful scenery. There are three courses in the Costa Azul, all also accessible from Lisbon. Local tourist offices have details of how to arrange a game.

Estoril and Cascais ★

Lisbon's twin seaside resorts are popular with day-trippers and are only 25 minutes away by train. Both have pleasant beaches. 'Night-trippers' too come to gamble and enjoy Las Vegas-style revues at Estoril's **casino**, the largest in Europe. **Estoril**, 13km (8 miles) south of Sintra and 24km (15 miles) west of Lisbon, is a quiet resort much favoured by **golfers**, who have six top-class courses to choose from within 25km (16 miles) of town.

Cascais, 6km (4 miles) further west, is the livelier resort of the two and everything is within walking distance. This small and pretty town has good shops, bars and restaurants and a maze of little streets, many pedestrianized. Watch the fishermen setting out their lobster pots on the quayside and then take a 30-minute stroll west to **Boca do Inferno** (Mouth of Hell) where the sea pours under an arch into a cave – it's at its most dramatic in stormy weather.

ESTREMADURA

Historic sights in central Portugal are scattered and there is little organized tourism, but the region is a rewarding one to explore. Take the time to stop and look around, leave the car and enjoy numerous walking opportunities, deserted beaches and tantalizing seafood restaurants.

Below: *The golden sands of Cascais make it a popular day trip for sun-seeking visitors; it's also a pleasant place to stay.*

Óbidos ★★

If you like your rural towns pretty as a picture, this is a natural stop. Stay overnight too if you can and savour the atmosphere. You won't be the first person to fall for Óbidos's charms – Dom Dinis gave it to his wife Isabel as a wedding gift in 1282 and, although she had the pick of Portugal, she loved to stay here.

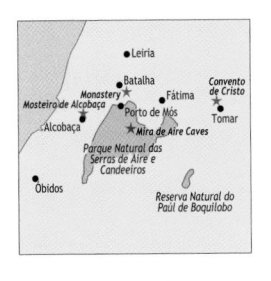

Left: *The narrow lanes of the medieval town of Óbidos are a delight to explore.*

The medieval **old town**, enclosed by walls, is simply charming to wander around. Note the fine *azulejos* on the inside walls of the **Porta da Vila**, the main gate. The interior of the **Igreja de Santa Maria** in Rua Direita is covered in blue 17th-century *azulejos* and contains some paintings by Josefa de Óbidos, a 17th-century woman artist. The **castle,** now converted into a deluxe *pousada*, is a fine example of the genre.

Alcobaça ★★

This otherwise unremarkable small town has one of Portugal's main architectural masterpieces, the **Mosteiro de Santa Maria de Alcobaça**. It's a 12th-century Cistercian monastery which, in its day, was one of the richest and most powerful in the country. Open daily 09:00–17:00.

The church demonstrates the clean lines and space of the best Cistercian architecture. The **tombs** of Dom Pedro and his mistress Inês de Castro face each other across the transept. The adjacent abbey buildings include elegant **cloisters**, with the lower storey dating from the 14th century and the upper one added, with typical Manueline features, in the 16th century.

Batalha Monastery ★★★

This atmospheric monastery is another architectural gem that demonstrates the flamboyant 15th-century late **Gothic** style with many **Manueline** additions. The exterior of the building is quite extraordinary – all flying buttresses, perpendicular spires, latticework windows,

MURDER MOST HORRID

Dom Pedro and Inês de Castro are Portugal's most famous pair of star-crossed lovers. Pedro fell in love with Inês, a Galician noblewoman, but was forbidden to marry her by his autocratic father, who feared her powerful family would influence affairs of state. They continued their affair until King Afonso had her murdered in Pedro's absence. When Pedro succeeded to the throne two years later in 1357 he rounded up the murderers, ripped out their hearts and ate them. As a follow-up he revealed he had secretly married Inês, exhumed her body and forced the court to pay homage to their queen by kissing her hand. The lovers are buried in Alcobaça's Mosteiro de Santa Maria.

Above: *There is a wealth of detail to be found on the elegant arches of Batalha's Royal Cloisters.*
Opposite: *The lovely tiles of Conimbriga's House of the Fountains date from the 2nd century AD.*

stained glass and gargoyles. The church interior is epic in size but quite plain; the **Capela do Fundador** to the right lies beneath a star-shaped dome. Here lie the tombs of João I and Philippa, his English queen, along with those of their four younger sons, including Henry the Navigator.

The **Royal Cloisters** fuse Gothic and Manueline style to great effect. Every arch carries carvings of shells, ropes, pearls and flowers. In the **chapter house**, glance upwards at the bold 20m (66ft) vault, an engineering feat which was considered so dangerous to build that only prisoners on death row worked on its construction. Note the outstanding Manueline detail on the pillars and the doorway of the **unfinished chapels** (Capelas Imperfeitas). Open daily 09:00–17:30.

EAST AND NORTH

On the road east to visit the former power base of the Knights Templar at **Tomar** you will skirt the northern fringes of the **Serra de Aire e Candeeiros**, a rugged limestone range which is a good spot for a picnic or walk. The largest cave system in Portugal is at **Mira de Aire**, around 14km (9 miles) southeast of Porto do Mós. You will also pass **Fátima**, the most important focus of pilgrimage in Europe after Lourdes, visited by four million people a year on the key dates of 12/13 May and 12/13 October.

Convento de Cristo ★★

On a hill overlooking Tomar and enclosed by 12th-century walls, this former headquarters of the Knights Templar looks more like a castle than a convent. The design of the 16-sided church was based on the **Church of the Holy Sepulchre** in Jerusalem and there are several cloisters. The unique feature of the Convento is the stunning **Manueline window** in the **chapter house**, embellished

---

THE MIRACLE OF FÁTIMA

In May 1917 three peasant children from Fátima witnessed an apparition of the Virgin Mary. The following October a crowd of devotees saw lights shooting from the sun and some were cured of their illnesses. The Virgin gave Lucia, the oldest child, three prophesies. The first outlined the prayers and sacrifices necessary to end World War I. The second was that Russia would be converted. The third remains secret and is apparently so explosive that only the Pope knows its content.

with the roots of a cork oak, the head of a sea captain and a bunch of seaweed as well as the more conventional anchors, ropes and flowers. Open daily 09:15–17:00.

Coimbra ★

This traditional university town, once the country's capital, enjoys a charming setting on the banks of the Mondego River. All the sites of interest are in a compact area just north of the river. The **Old Cathedral** or Sé Velha (open daily 10:00–18:00, closed Sunday) dates from the 12th century and the university, dating from the 16th century and one of the oldest in Europe, is housed in an impressive former palace (open daily 09:30–12:00 and 14:00–17:00). There's a huge ornate **library**, a Manueline **chapel** and a ceremonial hall for graduation. The **Museu Machado de Castro** (open 09:30–12:30 and 14:00–17:00, closed Monday) has an important collection of sculpture and paintings spanning the 14th–17th centuries.

The **Roman ruins of Conimbriga** (open 09:00–13:00 and 14:00–18:00, closed Monday) are the most extensive in Portugal and are located 16km (10 miles) southwest of town. Visit the **museum** first to get an idea of the layout and history of the site; the **excavations** do not really show how large and sophisticated a town this was in its heyday from the 1st to the 5th century AD.

SERRA DE ESTRELA

If you like your landscapes wild then a visit to the **Serra da Estrela**, the Mountains of the Stars, which rise to almost 2000m (6500ft), should be on your itinerary. Covered in snow in winter, the lonely upland moors are grazed by sheep. For information on walking routes, scenic drives and background on natural history you can buy English-language booklets at tourist offices in **Guarda** and **Covilhã**. Try to avoid driving at weekends when traffic jams block the narrow mountain roads.

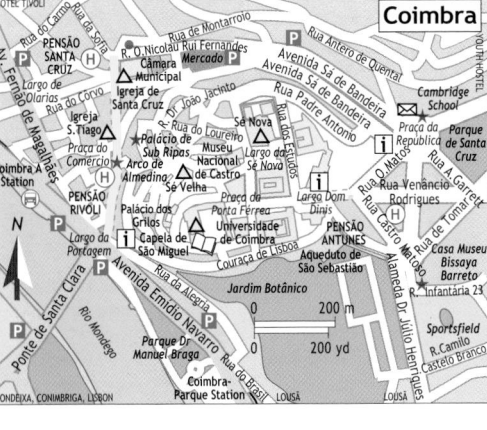

Around Lisbon and Central Portugal at a Glance

If you want to sunbathe and swim, then **Jun–Sep** is the best time – the Atlantic water will be at its warmest in August and September, but the former month is when the Portuguese decamp en masse to their favourite stretch of coast. **Winters** are mild except at elevation in the northeast; **spring** and **autumn** see pleasant daytime temperatures of around 15°C (60°F) and the bonus of wild flowers and autumn colours in the woods.

To get to Sintra from Lisbon, take a **train** from the Rossio station; the coastal service for Cascais and Estoril departs from Cais do Sodré. **Buses** to Setúbal, with onward connections to Sesimbra, leave from Lisbon's Praça de Espanha and from Oriente, the **metro** station for Parque das Nações. Óbidos, Tomar and Coimbra all have rail services. Lisbon's Santa Apolonia station serves destinations in central Portugal and the Rossio serves Estremadura. The region is also served by express buses from the capital.

Sintra, Mafra, Cascais/Estoril and seaside resorts just to the north are all connected by frequent local **bus** services. Óbidos, Batalha and Alcobaça can be visited by bus; if coming from Óbidos,

change at Caldas da Rainha. Leira is likewise the transport hub connecting Tomar with Batalha and Coimbra.

Sintra
LUXURY
Palácio de Seteais, tel: 21 923 3200, www.tivoli hotels.com Five-star, in antique-filled old palace with lovely grounds.

MID-RANGE
Quinta das Sequoias, tel: 219 230 342, www.quintadasequoias.com Beautiful manor house past the Palácio de Seteais.

BUDGET
Pielas, Avenida Desidero Cambournac 1, tel: 21 924 1691. Clean and friendly.
Quinta da Paderna, Rua da Paderna 4, tel: 21 923 5053. Near old town, pleasant views.

Cascais
MID-RANGE
Solar Dom Carlos, In an old mansion, lots of attractive tiles and garden. Rua Latino Coelho, Cascais, tel: 21 4828 115, www.solardomcarlos.com

Costa Azul
LUXURY
Pousada de Palmela, tel: 21 235 1226, www.pousadas.pt Within the castle building.
Pousada de São Filipe, Setúbal, tel: 265 523 844. Refurbished historic fortress.

MID-RANGE
Hotel do Mar, Sesimbra, tel: 21 228 8300, www.hoteldomar.pt Four-star, with sea views and indoor and outdoor pools.
Quinta das Torres, Azeitão, tel: 21 218 0001, fax: 21 219 0607. A 16th-century mansion in peaceful surroundings.

Óbidos
LUXURY
Pousada do Castelo, tel: 262 955 080, www.pousadas.pt Luxury hotel in old castle.

MID-RANGE
Casa do Poço, Travessa da Rua Nova, tel: 262 959 358. Atmospheric rooms ranged around a central courtyard.

Coimbra
LUXURY
Palace Hotel do Buçaco, tel: 231 937 970, www. almeidahotels.com A country residence north of Coimbra.

MID-RANGE
Hotel Tivoli, Rua João Machado, tel: 239 858 300, www.tivolihotels.com Near the bus station, with pool.

BUDGET
Dozens of pensions cater to student market; ask at Turismo.

Estoril
Hotel Inglaterra, Lovely cream-coloured old mansion, with pool. Rua do Porto, Estoril, tel: 21 4684 461, www.hotelinglaterra.com.pt

Around Lisbon and Central Portugal at a Glance

Tomar
LUXURY
Hotel dos Templários,
Largo Candido dos Reis,
tel: 249 310 100,
www.hoteldostemplarios.pt
New hotel with pool.

MID-RANGE
**Residencial Cavaleiros
Cristo**, Rua Alexandre
Herculano 7, tel: 249 321
203, www.inncavaleiros
decristo.com Central
location, nice decor.

Sintra
Tulhas Bar & Restaurante,
Rua Gil Vicente 4, tel: 21 923
2378. Good atmosphere and
regional dishes.

Cascais
Rua Flores. This street has a
good selection of restaurants
offering similar Portuguese
cooking and prices.

Sesimbra
Avenida 25 de Abril on the
waterfront is the best place to
go if you want fish – there are
lots of places to choose from.

Sintra
Ozono Mais, Rua General
Alves Roçades 10, tel: 219
619 927, www.ozonomais.
com Jeep tours and more.

Costa Azul
Vertigem Azul, Rua Praia
de Saude, Setúbal,

tel: 265 238 000,
www.vertigemazul.com
Canoe trips, dolphin watching.
Planeta Terra, 9 Praça
General Luis Domingues,
Setúbal, tel: 265 080 176,
www.planetaterra.pt
Week-long mountain
bike tours and jeep safaris.
Sal, Avenida Manuel Maria
Portela 40, Setúbal,
tel/fax: 265 227 685,
www.sal.pt Day walks.
Mil Andanças, Avenida Luisa
Todi 121, Setúbal, tel: 265
532 996, www.mil-andan
cas.pt Off-road jeep safaris.

Serra da Estrela
**Clube Nacional de
Montanhismo**, Rua da
Industria 31C, Covilhã, tel:
275 323 364, fax: 275 313
514. Mountaineering,
walking, skiing and riding
excursions.
Geopark, near Castelo
Branco, for more information
see www.naturtejo.com/pt
History, geology and nature
combine in this new park
near the Spanish border.
Some of the activities you will
find are themed walking
trails, riding, kayaking, bird-
watching and more.

Tourist Offices
Sintra: Praça República 23,
tel: 21 923 1157.
Estoril: Arcadas do Parque,
tel: 21 466 3813, fax: 21
467 2280.
Cascais: Rua Visconde da
Luz, tel: 21 486 8204.
Setúbal: Praça do Quebedo,
tel: 265 534 402.
Sesimbra: Largo da Marinha,
tel: 21 288 540.
Palmela: Castelo de Palmela,
tel: 21 233 2122.
Óbidos: Rua Direita, tel: 262
959 231.
Alcobaça: Praça 25 de Abril,
tel: 262 582 377.
Batalha: Praça Mouzinho
de Albuquerque, tel: 244
765 180.
Tomar: Avenida Dr Candido
Madureira, tel/fax: 249
329 823.
Coimbra: Largo Dom
Dinis, tel: 239 832 591;
Praça República, tel: 239
833 202.
Covilhã: Avenida Frei
Heitor Pintao, tel: 275
322 170.
Guarda: Edificio da
Camara Municipal, Largo
do Município, tel: 271
205 530.

GUARDA	J	F	M	A	M	J	J	A	S	O	N	D
AVERAGE TEMP. °C	4	5	8	10	13	17	20	20	17	12	7	4
AVERAGE TEMP. °F	40	42	46	50	55	63	68	68	62	54	45	40
RAINFALL mm	149	104	133	73	69	42	15	16	39	79	110	144
RAINFALL ins.	6	4.1	5.2	3	3	2	0.5	0.5	1.5	3.1	4.3	5.7
DAYS OF RAINFALL	15	12	15	10	11	7	3	4	7	10	14	17

4
The Algarve

Sunny, accessible and full of sporting opportunities and great beaches, the Algarve is Portugal's **playground**. In terms of land area it covers no more than an eighth of the country but nevertheless has more hotel rooms, apartments and villas for rent than the rest of Portugal. The big draw for the three million or so tourists who arrive every year is its pleasant **climate**, which is among the best in Europe. Add 27 top-class **golf courses** and many **tennis**, **watersports** and **riding** centres, and you have the perfect recipe for a sporting holiday at any time of the year.

More indolent visitors are drawn by the **beaches**. Washed by clean Atlantic waters and sheltered by sandstone cliffs west of Faro, they extend along almost the entire southern coast. The remote beaches of the west coast are dramatic, while in the east the landscape of sandbars and lagoons forms the **Ria Formosa Nature Reserve**.

But there is plenty of **history** to go with the golden sands. Many seaside towns have witnessed the comings of traders and empire builders, among them Phoenicians, Romans, Carthaginians and **Moors**. The Moors loved the Algarve and, when the rest of Europe was languishing in the Dark Ages, their capital, Silves, was internationally renowned as a city of scholarship and opulent wealth.

Nature-lovers will be in their element, both in the coastal zones of the Ria Formosa and **Parque Natural de Sudoeste Alentejano e Costa Vicentina** and in the wooded hills behind the coast. Holiday-makers rarely stir much beyond their sun loungers; make the effort and get a glimpse of what is still very much rural Portugal.

DON'T MISS

★★★ Lagos: enjoy the history and style of this popular resort.
★★★ Silves: soak up the myths and atmosphere that surround this striking castle.
★★★ Western Beaches: leave the crowds behind and explore a dramatic landscape.
★★★ Ria Formosa Nature Reserve: look out for rare birds, explore the unique ecology or just relax on an island beach.
★★ Cabo São Vicente: take a trip to the end of the known world.

Opposite: *Fishermen take to the sea at Albufeira, the largest resort in the Algarve.*

CLIMATE

The Algarve is characterized by hot sunny summers and mild winters. Rain is rare between June and September but you can expect rainy days any other time, particularly from November to March. Spring starts early and summer lingers well into October. Sea temperatures in the sheltered lagoons of the eastern Algarve are warmer than in the west.

FARO AND AROUND

The capital of the Algarve, Faro has a long history, but the majority of the buildings date from the 19th and 20th centuries as it was devastated by the Great Earthquake. Most of what's left is in the small Cidade Velha (Old Town), just south of the marina.

Faro Old Town ★★

Enter through the **Arco da Vilha** and the **Cathedral** (Sé) is straight ahead across the elegant square lined with orange trees. Built in 1251, the exterior is remodelled Romanesque and Gothic while the interior, with its gilded woodwork, has Renaissance and Baroque elements. Open 10:00–17:00, Monday–Saturday.

The 16th-century **Convent of Nossa Senhora da Assunção** behind houses the Archaeology Museum. Roman mosaics and a collection of *azulejos* are the most striking exhibits, while the graceful arches of the cloisters are worth seeing in their own right. Open Monday–Friday, 10:00–18:00 and 12:00–18:00 Saturday and Sunday.

Leaving the old town by the **Arco da Repousa**, cross the **Largo de São Francisco** and visit the **church** of the same name to view the fine Baroque **interior** with blue *azulejo* tiles depicting scenes from the life of St Francis. The main shopping streets are **Rua Vasco da Gama** and **Rua Santo Antonio**.

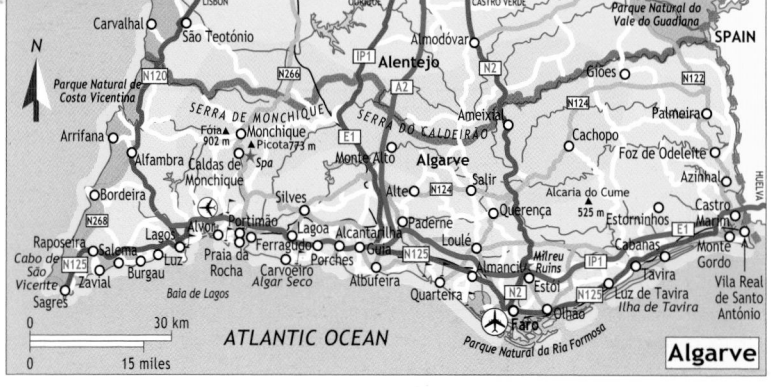

Milreu ★★

Here you'll find the most interesting **Roman remains** in the Algarve. The ruins date from the 1st century AD and comprise a large **country villa** with columns surrounding a central courtyard. On the west side was a **bathhouse** and on the east, the surviving wall of a **temple** to a local water deity. This was a sophisticated villa for its time and the standard of living the occupants enjoyed was superior to anything found in the Middle Ages, and probably higher than that experienced by isolated farmers even today. Open Tuesday–Sunday, 10:00–12:30 and 14:00–17:00.

Estói ★★

There's more evidence of stylish living at this nearby 18th-century aristocratic **palace**, currently being restored. But the **gardens** are wonderful, full of *azulejos*, nymphs, fountains and paths through the orange trees. Steps lead down to a **grotto** with statues of Diana, Venus and the Three Graces. Open Tuesday–Saturday, 10:00–12:30 and 14:00–17:00.

Above: *This charming nymph is one of the many neoclassical statues decorating the grounds of the Palace of Estói.*
Opposite: *A view of Faro's former Bishop's Palace from the bell tower of the Cathedral.*

Loulé ★★

Most visitors arrive on Saturday morning to visit the weekly **Gypsy Market**, but Loulé is a rewarding town to visit any day of the week. The Gypsy Market is a bit overrated unless you want to buy the usual tourist souvenirs and leather goods at prices higher than in many of the shops. The morning **Municipal Market** is held daily in the **Praça da República** and is just as interesting and a great place to buy delicious, organic fresh fruit and vegetables.

Loulé is a town where traditions of **craftsmanship** live on. You can see artisans working brass, copper, tin and wrought iron in the streets around the market. Pottery, candles, shoes, wicker furniture and harnesses are also made here. The **parish church** of **São Clemente** encapsulates a mixture of styles, ranging from 13th-century Gothic to later Manueline embellishments. The

> ### FARO'S HISTORY
>
> It was the Moors who gave Faro its name and developed it as a city. Faro was also their last important stronghold in Portugal, only capitulating to Christian forces in 1249 – a century after Lisbon's 'liberation'. In 1596, during Spain's 60-year rule of Portugal, Faro was sacked and set ablaze by English forces under Queen Elizabeth's favourite, the Earl of Essex. The city was rebuilt only to be destroyed again in the Great Earthquake of 1755.

Right: *The peaceful woods of the Fonte de Benemola are a great spot for a picnic or stroll.*

tall **bell tower** with its onion dome is all that remains of the former mosque, which was Christianized by placing the Portuguese coat of arms on the vault of the steeple.

Despite being a hard-working town, Loulé lets its hair down during **Carnival** – the five days of mayhem which precede Lent. You can expect fireworks, flower-covered floats, fancy dress, drinking and dancing in the streets – and also water and flour bombs aimed at friends which often miss their targets!

You're ideally placed at Loulé to do a couple of delightful **scenic drives** which showcase some of the Algarve's loveliest landscapes. Head a few miles east to the N2 road, follow it northwards and you will soon be climbing into the **Serra do Caldeirão**. The air is fragrant with the scent of pines and eucalyptus and alive with the sound of birdsong, and in spring wild flowers bloom in the meadows.

Alternatively, drive northeast to **Querença** and take the road to **Aldeia da Tor**, noting the remains of Moorish terracing on the hillside. Look out for a signpost to the **Fonte de Benemola**. If you want a short walk of 4km (2.5 miles), follow the track along the river and return, via stepping stones, along the opposite bank. The attractive village of **Salir**, where a once-mighty Moorish castle dominated the area, is a few miles to the north.

LOULÉ RITUAL

Altogether more solemn occasions than Carnival are the annual **Mãe Soberana** (Sovereign Mother) processions. On Easter Sunday a 16th-century statue of the Virgin with her dead son is carried from her shrine on a hillside into town. Two weeks later she is returned. Although full of Christian trappings and piety, this ceremony is a direct descendant of pagan rituals which celebrated the return of spring and the bounty of the Great Goddess.

Alte ★★

Alte enjoys a reputation as the 'prettiest village in the Algarve' and is full of spotless **cottages** with **patios** and **balconies** overflowing with flowers. The **church** has some attractive *azulejos* from Seville. A five-minute walk takes you to the **fonte** – a popular picnic spot by a stream. The two **restaurants** here stage folklore evenings in the summer – Alte is well known for its talented **traditional musicians**, singers and dancers.

FROM PRAIA DA FARO TO FERRAGUDO

Faro has its own beach, **Praia da Faro**, easily accessible by bus or (in summer) ferry. It's a pleasant spot with miles of sand, watersports and plenty of cafés and restaurants which are popular with the locals.

Further west are two of the most exclusive developments in the Algarve – **Quinta do Lago** and **Vale do Lobo**. Both offer superb tennis and golf facilities along with classy hotels, villas and apartments. The village of **Almancil** has a wide choice of expensive international restaurants and one of the Algarve's most interesting churches, **São Lourenço**, with its gilded altar and blue and white *azulejos*.

Thirty years ago **Quarteira** was a pretty fishing village but is at present, a jumble of high-rise apartment blocks which are used to house Portuguese hotel workers. Despite its rather less than perfect looks it has more of a Portuguese atmosphere than many more fashionable resorts, and is a good source of cheap accommodation. Next door is **Vilamoura,** a more upmarket development, with its marina, water sports, deep-sea fishing trips and golf courses.

Below: *You'll need a powerful shot to clear these ravines at Vale do Lobo.*

ALBUFEIRA'S HISTORY

Albufeira was an important port in Roman times and was called Baltum. In the 8th century the Moors renamed it al-Buhera – literally 'castle by the sea'. Over the next four centuries the town thrived thanks to trade links with North Africa. It was one of the last Moorish strongholds in Portugal, only falling to the Portuguese in 1250. With its trade links severed the town fell into decay; it was flattened by the Great Earthquake and then virtually destroyed by Miguelite supporters in the War of the Two Brothers.

Albufeira ★★

Albufeira is the largest resort on the Algarve, with a lively atmosphere and plenty to do throughout the year. Purists may claim it's all over-commercialized but it makes a fantastic base if you want to tour by car. The entire southern coast, from **Sagres** to **Vila Real**, lies in day-trip range.

The town has by no means lost all its original charm, and the best place to discover its past is to start off at **Praia dos Barcos**, Fisherman's Beach. Here fishermen unload their catch early in the morning, and mend their nets amid hordes of sunbathers later in the day. On the terrace above the beach are a clutch of lively **restaurants** and all that is left of the town's once-formidable **castle**, destroyed by the 1755 earthquake.

Walk up the **Rua Nova** and you're in the heart of the **Old Town**, with its steep cobbled streets and old houses. The **Misericórdia Chapel** in Rua Henrique Calado dates from the 16th century and is said to occupy the site of a mosque. The main shopping street is **Rua 5 de Outubro** and the centre of evening entertainment is **Largo Engenheiro Duarte Pacheco**, full of bars and fast-food restaurants. Just to the east of Albufeira are the satellite developments of **Montechoro** and **Praia da Oura**, connected to Albufeira by **The Strip** – a road running down to the sea which is lined with souvenir shops and bars. There's no old-town charm here but the beach is excellent.

If you like **chicken**, drive a mere 5km (3 miles) north of Albufeira to **Guia**, on a junction with the EN125. Here you'll find a dozen restaurants specializing in chicken piri piri – chicken barbecued in a delicious tangy chilli sauce. Many locals come from as far away as Faro on weekend evenings to eat here in large groups and debate the merits of one establishment over another.

Between **Armação da Pera** and Albufeira are the delightful

sandy beaches of **São Rafael**, **Praia do Castelo** and **Galé**, which are fast being developed as resorts in their own right. Galé is the centre for water and jet skiing. Armação itself is somewhat dowdy, but the coastline to the west is beautiful, with lots of little coves. **Algar Seco** is a noted beauty spot, a wonderfully dramatic outcrop of golden, ochre and russet cliffs, holed like a honeycomb with caves and passages.

Above: *The beach at Carvoeiro is one of the most photographed and painted in the Algarve.*

Opposite: *Albufeira is a modern resort, but it retains its some of its original charm.*

Carvoeiro ★★

This small resort was once an artists' colony, and it's still as pretty as a picture, despite the rash of villa development spreading over the surrounding hills. It can be extremely busy in the summer months but still makes a pleasant base.

Ferragudo ★★

Located on the banks of the estuary of the River Arade, Ferragudo retains plenty of its original charm, with its narrow streets and quaint houses. The local houses display traditional chimneys, door knockers and tiling. Walk along the beach beyond the 17th-century fort which once guarded the entrance to the harbour and you'll come to **Praia Grande** (Big Beach), one of the best spots in the Algarve for windsurfing.

VERNACULAR ARCHITECTURE

Aside from *azulejos*, the Algarve's Moorish heritage has left plenty of interesting features such as the filigree chimneys and door knockers shaped like tiny hands which ward off the Evil Eye. Flat roofs act as handy terraces for drying fruits and are protected by latticed walls, (*platibandas*), which allow air to circulate but prevent the fruit from blowing away. Even modern villas have an exotic Moorish look with decorative chimneys, latticework balconies and arched windows.

Above: *Even on a hot day there's a chill in the air at Alcantarilha's bone chapel.*
Opposite: *Silves' castle and cathedral overlook the modern town.*

INLAND FROM THE COAST

Porches is famous for its pottery and ceramic workshops and you can choose from traditional or contemporary designs. In a complete contrast **Alcantarilha**, 5km (3 miles) east, is renowned for the **bone chapel** attached to its parish **church**. The interior is composed of the bones and skulls of 1500 former parishioners. There are also three **water parks** in the area – ideal for a day of fun in the water. Take your pick from Aqualand, Slide and Splash, and Zoomarine.

Paderne ★★

This is a typical **country village** about 13km (8 miles) north of Albufeira. You can either drive or walk to the ruined sandstone **castle** – it's a round trip of 7km (4.5 miles). Built by the Moors, it was conquered in 1249 by Dom Afonso III. Today only the outer walls remain; within them are the remains of a Gothic **chapel**. The arched **bridge** spanning the river below is believed to date from Roman times. The tourist office in Albufeira can give you details of short **walks** in the area which pass through low-intensity farmland dotted with orange and olive groves and bright with poppies and bluebells in the spring.

Lagoa ★

On your way to Silves you may care to stop off in Lagoa, a sleepy little town which is the centre of the Algarve's **wine industry**. Unfortunately the wines produced locally do not match up to the fine quality of other Portuguese regions. A large **expatriate community** lives in the surrounding countryside and there's an excellent choice of **restaurants**, with prices cheaper than those on the coast. In front of the parish **church** with its Baroque façade is the **war memorial** which commemorates local men who died in the colonial wars in Goa, Guinea, Mozambique and Angola.

Silves ★★★

It's hard to believe that this sleepy country town on the banks of the Arade was once a rich and powerful city, described as 'stronger and ten times more remarkable than Lisbon'. Believed to have been founded by the Phoenicians (the Arade was formerly navigable), Silves has been settled since Palaeolithic times. Visit the fine **Archaeology Museum** on the Rua das Portas de Loulé to view some of the local finds. Open daily 10:00–19:00.

Arabs from the **Yemen** transformed Silves into one of the richest cities in Europe. Full of mosques, bazaars and palaces, it was likened to Baghdad. When the once-impregnable castle was captured by Christian forces in 1249, Silves fell into decline.

Silves has the best preserved **castle** in the Algarve. Its **turreted walls** dominate the town and provide panoramic views over the countryside. The peaceful **gardens** within reveal no hint of the savage hand-to-hand fighting which once took place, or indeed any hint of the Moors' presence aside from the deep well and vaulted roof of the **cistern** which led, via an underground passage, to the Arade River. Open daily 09:00–18:00.

The **cathedral** dates from the 13th century and was built on the site of the former mosque. It was once the leading cathedral in the Algarve and contains several crusader tombs.

WESTERN ALGARVE

Praia da Rocha was one of the first places in the Algarve to develop as a holiday resort and today it looks dated, with lots of fast-food restaurants and cheap apartment blocks. The **beach** is still glorious, however. **Alvor**, further west along the coast, is a better bet if you're looking for fishing village charm.

Portimão ★★

This is a busy commercial town rather than a resort, but is none the worse for that. It's a good spot for clothes shopping should your holiday wardrobe need updating. Shoes, belts, bags and casual fashions can be found in **Rua Vasco da Gama** and **Rua do Comércio**. For a crash course in Portuguese history, visit **Largo 1 de Dezembro** near the tourist office. The *azulejo*-backed benches depict key events from 1143–1910.

FISHING FRENZY

You don't have to be an experienced fisherman to take a big-game fishing trip from Portimão, but it helps if you're a good sailor as it takes two hours to reach the fishing grounds and the sea can sometimes be rough. The main quarry is shark – blue, copper and mako. Some of the big ones weigh in at over 100kg (220 lb). While waiting for the sharks to bite, you can cast handlines for bass, moray eels and rays.

Opposite: *Portugal's Lost King, Dom Sebastião, in a uniquely 1970s representation.*
Right: *Plump and straight from the sea – don't leave Portimão without enjoying a lunch of grilled sardines.*

The **port** is one of the main centres for big-game fishing, coastal cruises and boat trips up the Arade. Along the quayside under the old **bridge** are a clutch of **sardine restaurants** where you can enjoy a cheap and delicious lunch – very much a Portimão institution – and you'll find plenty of locals doing the same thing.

Lagos ★★★

Lagos has all the ingredients for a successful holiday – plenty of sights, good restaurants, trendy bars and excellent beaches in the area. It's a favourite with footloose youngsters from all over Europe in the summer. A good place to start your explorations is in front of the **statue** of Henry the Navigator in the **Praça da República** on the waterfront. Lagos was his base port for the Great Discoveries. Cross the road and turn right to the 17th-century fort, **Ponta da Bandeira**, to visit the interesting **museum** which maps the progress of the mariners and charts the growth of Portugal's maritime empire. Open Tuesday–Sunday, 09:30–17:00.

Back in the square, look out for the small arcade which marks the site of Europe's first **slave market**, an industry which Henry developed to finance his expeditions. Leave the square by Rua de São Gonçalo; on your left is the **Igreja de Santo António**. Plain from the outside, the interior is a riot of gold Baroque woodwork, including flocks of joyful cherubs.

In **Praça Gil Eanes** you can't miss an extraordinary modern statue which looks like a cross between a flowerpot man and a modern spaceman. In fact it is **Dom Sebastião**, who perished during his disastrous crusade to Morocco in 1578. You can see the window from where he addressed his troops in the **Church of the Misericórdia** in the Praça da República.

SLAVE TRADE

Henry the Navigator found the slave trade a useful way to finance his voyages of discovery. At first forcibly abducted from their villages, slaves were later obtained through local chiefs, who found the arrangement a profitable way of dealing with captives from intertribal warfare. The miserable trade grew as other European nations followed the Portuguese lead, and at its height during the 18th century between seven and ten million slaves were shipped out of Africa. The Marquês de Pombal emancipated Portuguese slaves in 1773, but it took almost a century before slave trading was finally abolished.

Above: *The beams from the lighthouse at Cape St Vincent are visible 90km (55 miles) out to sea.*

CABO DE SÃO VICENTE

Cabo de São Vicente supposedly got its name from a Spanish priest who was martyred in the 4th century. His remains were washed ashore on the rocky cape and a church was built on the spot, watched over by ten ravens. When St Vincent's remains were taken to Lisbon in the 12th century, the ravens went too, maintaining their vigil from the ship's rigging. This part of the coast has seen plenty of action – Christopher Columbus was shipwrecked here in 1476, Sir Francis Drake sacked Vila do Infante in his Spanish campaign in 1587, and the French defeated a British fleet here in 1693.

WEST OF LAGOS AND INLAND

The first beach west of Lagos is **Dona Ana**. It gets rather crowded in summer but is still very pretty with its weathered cliffs, grottoes and stacks. Further along **Luz**, **Burgau** and **Salema** are all former fishing villages which are busy being developed but still remain relatively peaceful places for a beach holiday. Take the road south of **Raposeira** for some genuinely secluded beaches, among them Zaival, Ingrina, Barranco and João Vez.

Sagres ★★

Windy and bleak, **Cabo de São Vicente** is the extreme southwesterly point of continental Europe and has a real end-of-the-world feel. To the Romans and those before them this is exactly what it was; beyond the cape lay the great unknown.

The walls of the **Fortaleza** (fortress) rise on the promontory on the southern tip of the Sagres Peninsula. This is where Henry the Navigator is said to have founded the **Vila do Infante**, his famous **school of navigation**, around 1420. The giant compass rose etched on stone possibly dates from this period. Sagres itself is a small town popular with travellers and surfers rather than package tourists, and a good base from which to explore the wild beaches of the west coast.

West Coast Beaches ★★

The wild and beautiful west coast beaches have been protected from the developers by the brisk Atlantic winds as much as by the formation of the **Costa Vicentina Natural Park**. The only people you are likely to meet on the miles of golden sands are the local fishermen, surfers in wetsuits and latter-day hippies.

Be careful when swimming as the Atlantic rollers are rough and there can be strong currents. Many of the beaches are only accessible on foot or by 4WD; however, **Arrifana**, **Bordeira**, **Amado** and **Castelejo** have better road access than most.

Monchique ★★

A day trip up into the shady hills makes for a refreshing change of scenery, especially on a hot summer's day. The waters of the little spa town of **Caldas de Monchique** have been famous since Roman times for their healing properties. Try to arrive either early or late in the day to miss the tour buses and savour the tranquil atmosphere. Local specialities you may like to buy include **honey** and *medronho*, the local schnapps-like firewater. You can drive right to the top of **Foia**, the Algarve's highest peak at 900m (2953ft). At one time, it's said, you could see Sintra from here. If you fancy a walk you can scale the more attractive peak of **Picota** on the opposite side of the valley in a 9km (5.5-mile) round trip. The market town of Monchique is a pleasant spot to stroll around; don't miss the Manueline doorway of the 16th-century parish **church** in **Rua da Igreja**.

Below: *The woods in the Serra de Monchique are largely composed of pine, chestnut, eucalyptus and cork oak trees.*

MARINE HARVEST

Only low-level traditional fishing methods are allowed in the Ria Formosa Nature Reserve. The barrier islands are important nurseries for fish such as bream and bass which spawn in the sheltered waters. Clamming has long been a way of life for fishing communities here. Some of the former salt pans have now been turned into fish farms, rearing shellfish, bream, bass and sole.

Below: *Tiled benches in Olhão depict key scenes in the port's history.*

EASTERN ALGARVE

The coastline here is quite different to that of the west and is made up of lagoons, sandbars and islands which form part of the **Ria Formosa Nature Reserve**. Apart from the far west this is the least commercialized part of the Algarve, although it does contain three modern resorts: **Monte Gordo**, **Cabanas** and **Manta Rota**.

Olhão ★★

This is the most important fishing port in the Algarve and a good place to enjoy a seafood lunch. The white-washed **cottages** have a touch of the kasbah about them, perhaps a legacy of long contact with the fertile fishing grounds off the Moroccan coast. Just at the back of the parish church, the **Igreja da Nossa Senhora do Rosario** in Avenida da República, is a tiny open chapel, **Nossa Senhora dos Aflitos**. Here fishermen's wives used to pray for the safe return of their menfolk. In a glass case are wax legs, arms and heads – votive offerings left by those in search of cures for ailments.

Left: *The Ria Formosa Nature Reserve is a welcome antidote to the over-development of much of the Algarve's coast.*

Ria Formosa Nature Reserve ★★★

This is one of the most important **wetland areas** in Europe and a visit to the **interpretation centre** (open daily, 09:30–12:30 and 14:30–17:30) just to the east of Olhão will provide you with a fascinating introduction to the unique ecology of the area.

First stop are large **aquariums** containing some of the key fish and molluscs to be found in the lagoons, along with a sad collection of confiscated bird traps and illegal fishing nets. Much of the centre's work is aimed at educating children in the hope that they will grow up to be more conservation-minded than their parents generation.

Then go on a self-guided **walking tour** which leads past **salt pans**, an old tuna boat and a working tide mill. At the bird hide you can view storks and waterfowl and then move on to the remains of a **Roman salt fish factory**. Algarve **water dogs**, a rare and ancient breed with webbed feet, are bred here and a visit to the kennels is a must for dog lovers. There's also a **bird clinic** (not open to the public) where injured eagles, owls and falcons are nursed back to health and released. Returning to the interpretation centre you walk through a sandy area shaded with umbrella pines. Keep your eyes down for a glimpse of a chameleon – the eastern Algarve is the only place in Europe apart from southern Spain where these charming lizards can be found.

SALT PANS

The eastern Algarve is where you'll see salt being extracted from sea water using methods which have not changed much for thousands of years. Sea water is directed into giant pans, each the size of a football pitch. After impurities have dropped to the bottom, the water is moved to evaporation pans where the remaining water evaporates under the strong sun, leaving slushy salt crystals. These are raked out and left to dry. Former salt pans make an excellent habitat for birds.

Above: *There's plenty of fascinating detail to discover in the doorway of Tavira's Misericórdia church.*

ALGARVE WATER DOG

Look out for these distinctive rough-haired dogs on your travels – they are currently enjoying a new lease of life as pets, guard dogs and customs sniffer dogs. Formerly they were bred by fishermen and would guard the catch, chase fish into nets, deliver messages between boats, and even save sailors from drowning. One of the oldest European breeds, they almost became extinct after the 1974 revolution but numbers are now increasing as their friendly nature and robust constitution wins them new admirers.

Tavira ★★★

This elegant little town, which lies approximately 30 km (19 miles) from Faro, would make an ideal base to stay. The foundations of the stone arched **bridge** over the **River Gilão** date back to Roman times, and the town developed during the Moorish occupation. Most of the fine buildings date from the late 18th century as Tavira was badly damaged in the Great Earthquake. There are many pleasant **parks** dotted around town.

The 16th-century **Church of the Misericórdia** in Rua da Galeria has a fascinating doorway. The carved heads include the **Green Man**, an ancient fertility symbol surrounded by vines and vegetation. Among the saints and angels are sea horses, mermen and what looks very much like a rock guitarist, complete with electric leads trailing from his guitar.

Tavira's **beach,** the **Ilha de Tavira,** is on an offshore island. Take a bus to the ferry terminal, make the short crossing and then decide whether to hang out with the crowds on the inshore side with its rickety beach bars and restaurants, or head for the seaward side if you want to be alone.

AROUND TAVIRA

On your way between Olhão and Tavira, stop in **Luz de Tavira** and admire the ornate Manueline side door to the parish church. The town's coastal satellite, **Santa Luzia**, is the **octopus** capital of the Algarve and the **earthenware pots** on the quayside are a clue to how they are caught; they are laid on the sea bed, the octopuses crawl in under the impression they have found a nice secure hidey-hole, and the rest is history. The more adventurous can try some air-dried and grilled tentacles with a drink in the seafront cafés.

Driving just a few miles inland will take you into the semi-wild rolling hills of the **Serra de Alacaria do Cume**. A short circular drive of 25km (16 miles) will give you a flavour of the area. Take the Fonte Salgada turn-off from the EN125 which skirts Tavira, follow the signs to **Estorninhos** and then turn right to return to the coast. **Hay** is still gathered by hand on the steep hills and secured in little stooks. The curious round buildings with conical roofs are **hay lofts**. The design has not changed much since the Bronze Age and, interestingly, many modern houses in the area also feature conical roofs. Old habits die hard in this traditional area.

Vila Real ★

Submerged by the sea after the earthquake and rebuilt by the Marquês de Pombal along a grid system in just five months, Vila Real is architecturally like nowhere else in the Algarve and closely resembles the **Baixa** district in **Lisbon**. The central square, the **Praça de Pombal**, has a striking black and white mosaic pavement; glance down to admire the fish motifs on the wrought-iron drains. The Guadiana River marks the boundary with Spain and you can take a boat trip up the river to **Alcoutim** from here; it's also a pleasant trip on country roads by bike.

Castro Marim ★★

Just 3km (2 miles) north of Vila Real lies a tiny village dominated by a massive hilltop **castle** built by Dom Afonso III in the 13th century. The ruins are all that are left after the earthquake of 1755. Within the walls are the remains of a smaller castle which was once the head-quarters of the Order of Christ, as the Knights Templar renamed themselves. Also within the castle walls is an office where you can pick up a map of the surrounding nature reserve. Look out for flamingoes, storks, sandpipers and plovers.

> **KNIGHTS TEMPLAR**
>
> The Templars were a religious order of knights, formed in Jerusalem in the 12th century to fight infidels and protect Christians. Both the reigning powers and the Church became jealous of their plundered wealth and arrogance. Some said they practised the Black Arts and certainly many were well versed in Hermetic philosophy picked up in the Middle East. Many of the more lurid stories emerged under torture so can be discounted. They were excommunicated by the Pope in the 14th century but immediately relaunched themselves in Portugal under a new name, the Order of Christ.

Below: *The walls of Castro Marim's ruined castle overlook a nature reserve.*

The Algarve at a Glance

The Algarve is popular all year round by virtue of its excellent climate. When northern Europe shivers through the **winter** it's possible, if not perhaps to sunbathe, at least to enjoy lunch or a game of tennis or golf in shirt sleeves. As it's so far south (Faro is on the same latitude, 37°N, as Tunis, Sicily and southern Greece) the sun is always agreeably high. Having said that, rain is always a possibility in the winter and you should pack a warm jacket to cope with the odd bout of chilly weather. Many regulars rate **spring** (March to May) as the best time to visit; it's warm rather than hot, the wild flowers are lovely and the threat of rain is receding. **Summers** are hot but there is generally a cooling breeze on the coast. September and October are generally warm and occasionally even quite hot, but evenings can start to become a bit cooler.

There are direct flights to Faro from many European capitals, operated by charter as well as scheduled airlines.If arriving from Spain, Seville is 170km (105 miles) from Vila Real on a fast motorway. **TAP Air Portugal** and **Portugalia** both operate several flights a day from Lisbon to Faro. Faro is four hours from Lisbon by express **bus** and five hours by **train**. Change at Tunes if you're heading to Lagos by rail. Less frequent bus and rail connections link Faro with Oporto, Évora and Seville. For rail timetables *see* www.cp.net, for bus timetables *see* www.rede-expressos.pt or www.eva-bus.com.net

Bus services link most of the major towns, and timetables are posted at bus stops (for local services) and bus stations. Tourist offices often have details. **Trains** run from Vila Real in the east to Lagos in the west. Most services stop at all 47 stations in between, so get an express service if you are in a hurry. Some stations (e.g. Albufeira and Silves) are located some distance from the centre of town; those at Vila Real, Tavira, Faro, Portimão and Lagos are more convenient. The **car hire** scene is very competitive and rates are lower than in other parts of Portugal; as well as all the international companies, local firms include: **Auto Jardim**, tel: 291 524 023, www.autojardim.com **Rentauto**, tel: 289 818 718.

With such a huge choice of accommodation available, you may find it helpful to enlist the aid of the local tourist office in making your selection. Listed here are a few of the highlights.

Tavira
MID-RANGE
Mares Residencial, Rua Dr Jose Pires, Padinha 134, tel: 281 325 860. Central location, with good restaurant attached. **Quinta do Caracol**, São Pedro, tel: 281 322 475, fax: 281 323 175. This is an old converted farmhouse situated just outside town.

Faro
MID-RANGE
Hotel Eva, Avenida da República, tel: 289 001 000, fax: 289 802 304. This four-star hotel faces the marina.

Loulé
MID-RANGE
Hotel Loulé Jardim, Largo Dr Manuel Arriaga, tel: 289 413 094, fax: 289 463 177. Set in a quiet square, with a small pool.

Albufeira
LUXURY
Sheraton Pine Cliffs, Pinhal do Concelho, tel: 289 500 102, www.pinecliffs.com Stylish Portuguese decor with golf and other activities on the doorstep.

Silves
MID-RANGE
Hotel Colina dos Mouros, Pocinho Santo, tel: 282 440 420. A three-star hotel with a pool and stunning castle views.

Praia da Rocha
LUXURY
Hotel Bela Vista, tel: 282 450 480, fax: 282 416 379. Converted mansion right on the seafront, very popular.

The Algarve at a Glance

Lagos
MID-RANGE
Residencial Marazul, Rua 25 de Abril 13, tel: 282 770 230, fax: 282 769 960. Very central, with friendly staff.

Sagres
LUXURY
Pousada do Infante, Rua Antonio Faustino, tel: 282 620 240, www.pousadas.pt Elegant surroundings and good restaurant.

WHERE TO EAT

There's plenty of choice in most Algarve resorts – from traditional Portuguese cuisine to pizza, pasta, Chinese and Indian. Here are a few of the restaurants offering that elusive 'something different'.

Carvoeiro
A Fonte, Escandhinas Vai Essar 4, tel: 282 356 707. Portuguese fare, charcoal-grilled fish and meat, pleasant outdoor terrace.

Lagos
A Lagosteira, Rua 1 de Maio 2, tel: 282 762 486. Upmarket restaurant where prawns, lobster and cataplana are the house specials.

Olhao
Choose from a clutch of restaurants with sea views: Pappy's, Isidro, Cervejaria Ria, A Bote, and Formosa are worth trying.

Sagres
Vilha Velha, tel: 282 624 788. Offers a new take on traditional Portuguese cooking.

Quarteira
O Jacinto, Avenida Sa Carneiro, tel: 289 301 887. Top-class fish restaurant.

Querença (near Loulé)
Moinho ti Casinha, tel: 289 438 108. Traditional meat dishes in the countryside.

Praia do Faro
Camané, tel: 289 817 539. Fresh fish by the sea, much frequented by celebrities.

TOURS AND EXCURSIONS

Riosul, Monte Gordo, tel: 281 510 200, www.riosultravel.com Boat trips up the Guadiana and jeep tours in Eastern Algarve.
Horizonte, Salema, tel: 282 695 920. Environmentally focused jeep tours of the west coast.
Megatur, Rua Conselheiro de Bivar 80, Faro, tel: 289 807 485. Organized excursions to all corners of the Algarve.
Almargem, tel: 289 412 959, phone for details of the Saturday walks organized by this environmental group.
Peninsular, Vila Real, tel: 281 543 561, www.peninsular.cjb.net Fun trips up the Guadiana.

USEFUL CONTACTS

Tourist Offices
Albufeira: Rua 5 de Outubro, tel: 289 585 279.
Alcoutim: Rua 1 de Maio, tel: 281 546 179.
Carvoeiro: Largo Praia do Carvoeiro, tel: 282 357 728.
Faro: Rua da Misericórdia 8–12, tel: 289 803 604.
Lagos: Largo Marquês de Pombal, tel: 282 763 031.
Loulé: Avenida 25 de Abril, tel: 289 463 900.
Monchique: Largo dos Choroes, tel: 282 911 189.
Olhão: Largo Sebastião Martins Mestre, tel: 289 713 936.
Portimão: Avenida Zeca Afonso, tel: 282 416 556.
Praia da Rocha: Avenida Tomas Cabreira, tel: 282 419 132.
Quarteira: Avenida Infante de Sagres, tel: 289 389 209.
Sagres: Rua Commandante Matoso, tel: 282 624 873.
Silves: Rua 25 de Abril, tel: 282 442 255.
Tavira: Rua da Galeria 9, tel: 281 322 511.

FARO	J	F	M	A	M	J	J	A	S	O	N	D
AVERAGE TEMP. °C	12	13	14	16	18	22	24	24	23	19	16	13
AVERAGE TEMP. °F	54	55	58	61	65	72	75	75	73	66	61	55
HOURS OF SUN DAILY	6	6	6	6	7	8	8	8	7	7	6	6
RAINFALL mm	70	52	72	31	21	5	1	1	17	51	65	67
RAINFALL ins.	2.8	2.1	2.8	1.2	0.8	0.2	–	–	0.7	2	2.6	2.6
DAYS OF RAINFALL	9	7	10	6	4	1	–	–	2	6	8	9

5
The Alentejo

If you're looking for the 'real' Portugal there can be few better places to start your exploration than the Alentejo. This vast and sparsely populated **rural province** takes up a third of Portugal's land area but contains only a tenth of its population. It's equally accessible from Lisbon in the north and the beaches of the Algarve to the south. In between you'll find a stark landscape which is baked by the sun to shades of ochre and gold in summer and carpeted by wild flowers in spring. Huge fields of ripening **wheat** ripple to the horizon and most of the rest of the countryside is devoted to rough **pasture** for sheep and pigs, interspersed with ancient groves of **olive** and **oak**. The best way to discover the landscape is to leave your car and explore the dirt roads and tracks by mountain bike, horse or on foot.

All along the Spanish border country towns are crowned by great medieval **castles,** and **Évora** is a UNESCO World Heritage Site because of its extraordinary wealth of monuments which date from Roman times onwards; there are some outstanding megalithic monuments just outside the city.

The province is divided into two sections: the **Alto** (upper) **Alentejo** to the north and the **Baixa** (lower) **Alentejo** which borders the Algarve. Whatever your interest – history, nature, photography or wine (local vintages are among the best in the country) – you should find plenty to occupy yourself here. And you'll have the satisfaction of visiting one of the most distinctive but least known areas in Western Europe.

Opposite: *Wide horizons and drought-resistant vegetation characterize the Alentejo.*

Above: *Évora's fine Roman temple was walled in and used as a slaughterhouse in the 19th century before being restored.*
Opposite: *Figures of the apostles decorate the entrance to Évora's Cathedral.*

ÉVORA

Culturally, historically and politically important for centuries, Évora is a must-see on any itinerary. During the Middle Ages it was a centre of scholarship and the arts, attracting painters, architects, sculptors and writers. The **university** dates from 1557. If arriving by car, park it outside the old town and explore on foot. First stop should be the **Largo Marquês de Marialva**, which has the greatest concentration of monuments.

Temple of Diana ★★★

Built in the 2nd century AD, this is the best preserved Roman monument in Portugal, although the marble plinths and 14 granite Corinthian columns are all that remain. It was partially destroyed during the persecution of pagans by Christians in the 5th century.

Cathedral ★★

A large ostentatious building and a good example of the **transitional** period between **Romanesque** and **Gothic** architecture, the cathedral dates from 1186. The two towers are later additions and the high altar and choir stalls were remodelled in Renaissance style in the 16th century. (Open Tuesday–Sunday, 09:00–12:00 and 14:00–17:00.) Next door is the former **palace** of the powerful Archbishop of Évora, an impressive building in its own right and now housing a regional **museum** containing Neolithic, Roman and medieval finds along with some lovely *azulejos*. (Open 10:00–12:30 and 14:00–17:30; closed Monday.)

Also in the square is the **Convento dos Lóios**, a 15th-century monastery now enjoying a new lease of life as a *pousada*. The adjoining church of **São João Evangelista** contains some lovely *azulejos* but is not always open; check with the tourist office about the possibility of a guided visit. Next door, the **Palace of the Dukes of Cadaval** dates from the 14th century.

Church of Nossa Senhora da Graça ★

The four giant figures which dominate the **façade** of the Church of Our Lady of Grace have excited much speculation as to their significance. Some say the giants, each holding a globe, represent Portugal's domination of the four corners of the earth. A darker explanation suggests that the giants represent sub-human monsters burned by the **Inquisition**; Évora was one of the leading centres of this brutal period of religious persecution.

Church of São Francisco ★★

The main church dates from the 15th century but the big attraction is the **Capela dos Ossos** or Bone Chapel. This is faced with bones and skulls which belonged to over 5000 monks. An eerie inscription over the entrance reads, 'We bones here are awaiting yours'. Enter through a side chapel, where an image of the suffering Christ is dressed in Portuguese workman's clothes. Take a look at the glass panel on the left which is full of wax offerings in the shape of legs, arms and heads. These have been blessed in the hope that afflictions will be cured. Open daily, 10:00–12:45 and 14:30–17:45.

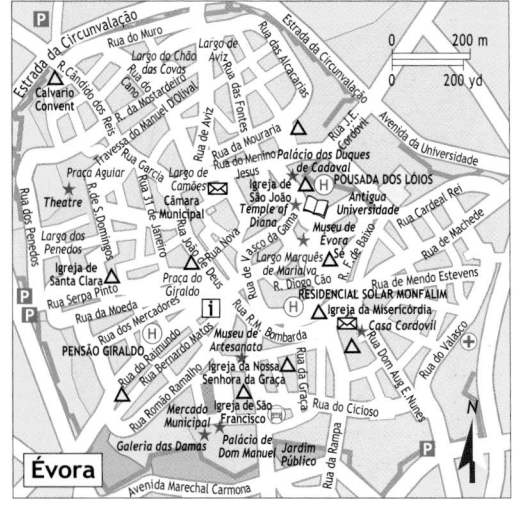

The Alentejo, with its rich landowners and poor agricultural workers, has always been one of the strongholds of the Communist party. After the 1974 revolution many landowners fled to Spain and Brazil, and the estates were taken over by the workers with much jubilation and turned into co-operatives. What happened next depends on who is telling the story. One version says that the ignorant peasants killed and ate most of the breeding stock and sold the rest, along with machinery, for a song. Without firm guidance the estates went to rack and ruin. In the other version the workers, despite great efforts, lacked the technical know-how to make the estates profitable. Many of the farms are now back in the hands of the original owners, who have returned from exile.

The town walls are built on top of Roman fortifications and extend through the pleasant **Jardim Público** (public gardens). The aqueduct in the northern part of the city dates from the mid-16th century.

AROUND ÉVORA

This fascinating trip around some of Évora's outstanding **prehistoric monuments** will take you into some lovely countryside; pack a picnic lunch and make a day of it. The Alentejo has been inhabited for many thousands of years. Megalithic construction of **dolmens**, **menhirs** and **stone circles** reached a peak in the 3rd and 4th millennia BC. Hiring a mountain bike would be a pleasant way to do this tour; many of the country lanes are on packed earth, although these should not present too much of a problem to cars except after heavy rain.

Below: *The Alentejo's countryside is well worth exploring by foot, horse or mountain bike rather than by motor car.*

Turn left off the N114 road from Évora to **Montemor-o-Novo** after 10km (6 miles) – it's signposted to Guadalupe. Continue on to **Valverde,** follow the signs to **Anta do Zambujeiro** and park at the agricultural research station belonging to the University of Évora. Across the stream you'll see a huge dolmen sheltered by a corrugated roof.

Anta do Zambujeiro ★★

This is the largest **dolmen** in Europe. The support stones of the chamber are 6m (20ft) in height and weigh several tons. The huge **capstone** was removed by archaeologists to prevent further cracking. Originally a burial chamber, the dolmen later became a centre of **cult worship**. Flint arrow heads, ceramic pots, amber beads and copper tools which were found here are on display at the Museum of Évora.

Now retrace your route back to Guadalupe and follow the signs for the **Cromeleque dos Almendres**. When you reach a group of farm buildings, **Monte dos Almendres**, park by the abandoned well and head diagonally across the field towards the grain silos, noting the tiled threshing floor on your left. Here is the **Menhir dos Almendres** – a phallic stone around 4m (13ft) high with engravings near the top.

Above: *The Cromeleque dos Almendres is one of the most important stone circles in Europe.*

Continue along the sandy road, passing through a lovely oak wood. The landscape has a melancholic air and gives the impression of great antiquity. Stop by the picnic table and you will see a stone circle on your left.

Cromeleque dos Almendres ★★★

This **stone circle** consists of 95 stones, with smaller circles contained within the main perimeter. It is thought to date from 2000BC and may have been used for astronomical calculations. Some of the stones have spiral and geometric **symbols** carved on their faces. Although its original purpose is unclear, the circle has been used for magical and religious **ceremonies** for millennia. The whole place has a magical feel to it; the woods are a lovely spot for a picnic, and Évora can be seen on the horizon.

If you have time, return to Valverde and turn right; beyond the village of **São Brissos** you will see a smaller **dolmen** which has been incorporated into the tiny village chapel. Take a right turn before **Santiago do Escoural** and follow the signs for Gruta do Escoural. This cave contains charcoal **etchings** of bison and horses made by Cro-Magnon artists some 15,000 years ago. Open Wednesday–Sunday, 9:00–12:00 and 13:30–17:30. Continue along the road to return to the N114.

> **FEEL THE FORCE**
>
> Some visitors to the Almendres Stone Circle have noticed a powerful force field emanating from the sandstone monolith with spirals and circles engraved on its face, located just off-centre. Try it yourself by standing around 2m (6ft) from the stone. The effect varies from nothing much to definite spine-tingling depending on individual sensitivity, or perhaps the fluctuations of the force itself. You could also experiment with walking between the gateways formed by pairs of stones.

Right: *Olives from the ancient groves of trees that thrive in the Alentejo.*

ALENTEJO AGRICULTURE

It was Julius Caesar who introduced *latifundias* – large estates devoted to cattle raising and wheat farming – to the Alentejo. Many of the boundaries of these estates have remained the same over the intervening 2000 years. The farmhouse itself is called a *monte* and is usually located on the highest point of the estate. Cork and olives are still produced in great quantities but wheat is no longer profitable – it's cheaper to import it from Spain where greater mechanization has cut production costs. The exodus from the land continues and the population has declined in the last 50 years by almost half to around half a million. In the past decade horticulturalists from northern Europe have set up small-scale fruit and vegetable operations which take advantage of the long growing season.

Viana do Alentejo ★★

This is the first stop on a circular tour after following the arrow-straight Roman road south from Évora. Inside the castle walls, with their sturdy ramparts resembling four circular towers, is a church. The walls are crenellated like the castle's with fake cannons pointing outwards and plenty of grotesque gargoyles. The doorway is a fine example of Manueline style, with lots of swirls and embellishments.

Alvito ★

The powerful barons of Alvito built the **castle** here in 1494. It's now a *pousada,* and guests dine in the **Great Hall** where the barons once entertained their royal guests. Around town look out for examples of ornate Manueline stonework on arches, balconies and windowsills. The parish **church** is a handsome 15th-century sandstone building with crenellated walls and a sundial.

Portel ★

Almost exactly equidistant between Évora and Beja, Portel was granted its royal charter in the 13th century and the handsome castle, flags fluttering in the breeze, dates from the same period.

Freixo Dolmens ★

Returning to Évora along the IP2, turn left into the village of **São Manços** and take another left at the signpost to **Torre de Coelheiros**. On the outskirts of the village turn right at the manor house onto a signposted track. Park by the reservoir and follow the stream to the first **dolmen**; the second is larger and lies to the southwest across a wheatfield.

ESTREMOZ

On the way from Évora to Estremoz, the castle of **Évora-Monte** is an unmistakable sight from the road. It looks like a giant sandcastle and is a modern reconstruction of the original, built by **Dom Dinis** in 1312.

Estremoz itself is one of the most rewarding and atmospheric towns to visit in the Alentejo. It has plenty of **royal connections** and was the focus of several decisive military campaigns against the Spanish. Best place to start is the **Rossio**, the central square. There's a **traditional market** here every Saturday, which is a great place to buy the typical red Estremoz **pottery** or hand-painted **ceramics** at reasonable prices.

The **tourist office** is on Largo Republica around the corner from the town hall. Take a look inside the latter (it was a convent in the 17th century) and admire the fine *azulejos* which run up the staircase. For a close encounter with Alentejano **farmers**, pop into **Café Alentejano**, full of old-timers in flat hats discussing the weather and the price of feed. At the bar, pride of place is taken by a whole roast suckling pig destined to be carved into *bifanas* – hot pork rolls. To the northwest of the square is **Lago da Gadhana**, an ornamental lake with a statue of Saturn bearing his scythe in the centre.

Below: *The striking castle of Évora-Monte was where the War of the Two Brothers was concluded with the signing of a peace treaty.*

Torre das Três Coroas ★★★

The **walls** survive but all that remains of the 13th-century royal castle is the **tower**. Built of grey marble and 27m (89ft) high, it was known as the **Tower of the Three Crowns** because it was built by three kings: Sancho II, Afonso III and Dom Dinis. After the death of Dom Dinis the adjoining **royal palace** was used as an ammunition dump, but it exploded in 1698. What is left has been converted into a luxurious *pousada*.

Through the grille of the tiny **chapel** of Santa Isabel you can see *azulejos* depicting the life of the saintly Queen Isabel, Dom Dinis' wife. This was the room in which she died. The **Municipal Museum** is in the same square and contains clay figurines depicting peasant life and religious themes, along with old firearms and furniture. Displayed upstairs is a reconstruction of a typical country kitchen. Open Tuesday–Sunday, 09:00–12:15 and 14:00–17:15.

VILA VIÇOSA AND ALONG THE SPANISH BORDER

On the way here from Estremoz, you can't fail to notice the huge marble quarries just outside the town of

Borba. The marble produced here is among the best in the world and much is exported to Italy. Leftover chips are heated in an earth oven to produce the whitewash (*cal*) used to paint houses, with oxides added for blue and ochre shades.

Vila Viçosa itself is a pleasant town and many of the houses have fine marble doorways and windowsills. The **Praça da República**, paved with marble and lined with orange trees, is where you'll find both the **castle** and the **tourist office**.

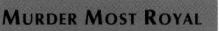

Left: *Statue of Dom João IV with the Paço Ducal in the background.*

Opposite: *The chapel of Queen Isabel stands on the site of her former palace.*

Castle ★★

The castle, built by the ubiquitous Dom Dinis in the 13th century, was restored in the 16th century in the Italian style which was then in vogue. It has seen plenty of action over the centuries, having defended the town against both Spanish and Napoleonic forces. Within the castle is a **Museum of Hunting** which is stuffed full of trophies. The curator will show you around, proudly pointing out extinct species. Open daily, 09:30–13:00 and 14:00–17:30.

Paço Ducal ★★★

This monolithic **palace** in grey and ochre marble dominates a great square containing an equestrian statue of Dom João IV, the first Bragança to gain the throne after the period of Spanish rule came to an end in 1640. The palace was built in 1573 for the powerful dukes of Bragança. Even after the family had their pick of sumptuous palaces in Lisbon and Sintra they retained an affection for Vila Viçosa.

Tour guides will show you round the collections of oriental tapestries, porcelain, paintings and frescoes bequeathed to the nation by the last king of Portugal, who died in exile in London in 1932. The kitchens claim to have the largest collection of copper pots in Europe and there is also an armoury featuring weaponry from medieval times onwards. Open Tuesday–Sunday, 09:30–13:00 and 14:30–17:30. The adjoining 16th-century monastery is now a newly refurbished *pousada*.

MURDER MOST ROYAL

In 1512 one of the Duke of Bragança's men passed on to his master the news that a young man was secretly visiting the Duchess by night when he was away from the palace. The Duke kept watch in the garden, and his suspicions were confirmed when he spotted a boy about to climb through one of the upstairs windows. The Duke shouted a threat, causing the young man to fall to his death. He then confronted his wife, who protested her innocence but to no avail; the enraged Duke hacked her to death with his broadsword. Too late he discovered that the young man, a page, had been visiting one of the Duchess' ladies-in-waiting.

Elvas ★★

Elvas is a frontier town par excellence, fortified to the maximum with moats, forts, walls, ramparts and gates. The best views of the fortifications are from the **castle**, which houses a small **Military Museum** (open daily, 10:00–13:00 and 14:00–17:30). On the way take a look inside the **Igreja de Nossa Senhora da Consolação** in the pleasant cobbled square, **Largo de Santa Clara**. Plain on the outside, the interior of the church is covered with 17th-century *azulejos*. The square features a Moorish archway and a pillory to which criminals were chained.

Castelo de Vide ★★

This hilltop **village** was once home to a sizeable Jewish community, and the **Judiaria** area to the south of the **castle** is the most picturesque part of town, full of white cottages and cobbled lanes. The castle itself was built by Dom Dinis in the 13th century. Have a refreshing drink of water at the **Fonte de Vila** (town fountain); the natural mineral water is said to be good for the blood and kidneys.

Marvão ★★

From this clifftop eyrie, the views east over the Spanish mesa and north to the peaks of the Serra da Estrela alone make a visit here worthwhile. The 13th-century **castle** is built into the cliff face and was virtually impregnable. Marvão was first fortified by the Moors and from 1640 to 1660 was relentlessly attacked by Spain.

Monsaraz ★★

This little village, perched on a steep hill and visible for miles around, is one of the most atmospheric places in the Alentejo. Cobbled lanes, old houses and the obligatory

DAMMED SPOT

The Barragem de Alqueva to the west of Reguengos de Monsaraz, where the Guadiana has been dammed, is the biggest artificial lake in Europe, 85km (52 miles) long with a 1200km (745-mile) shoreline. It was built to alleviate the Alentejo's chronic water shortages. The villages of Alqueva, Amiera and Estrela on the new lake shore now offer sailing, fishing and canoeing trips. However, Friends of the Earth has condemned the scheme as 'the biggest ecological crime ever committed in Portugal', claiming that the damage done to the environment and wildlife of the Guadiana valley outweighs any benefits.

castle combine to make you feel you've stepped back in time to medieval days. Monsaraz has been inhabited since prehistoric times and has many interesting remains just outside town – among them the **Menhir de Bulhoa**, the dolmen of **Olival da Pega** and the **Xarez** stone circle. On the Reguengos road, the village of **São Pedro do Corval** is a good place to buy ceramics.

BAIXA ALENTEJO

The southern part of the Alentejo may not have quite as much historical interest as the north but it still has plenty of character and some rewarding sights.

Serpa ★★

If arriving by car, try to park before entering the **old town**, as otherwise you'll encounter tight corners, blind bends and lanes so narrow you'll think (with some justification) that your car will jam. The main square, the **Praça da República**, has a good choice of cafés; you may be lucky enough to be serenaded by a band of the town's **traditional singers**. Clad in sheepskin and with vivid woven bags and blankets thrown over their shoulders, they are genuine descendants of medieval troubadours. Their haunting songs have Moorish cadences and have been handed down over generations.

The **castle** was very badly damaged in the **Spanish War of Succession** in 1707, it is open Tue–Sun, 09:00–12:30 and 14:00–17:30. The **Ethnographic Museum** in Largo do Corro presents aspects of Alentejano rural life, unfortunately without any English explanations. Open Tue–Sun, 09:00–12:30 and 14:00–17:30. Just outside the town, next to the *pousada*, is the small Moorish-style **Capela de São Gens**, which was once a mosque.

Opposite: *You need good legs to tackle the steep uphill approaches to Monsaraz.*
Below: *Glance upwards and you'll spot these distinctive lamps in Serpa's main square.*

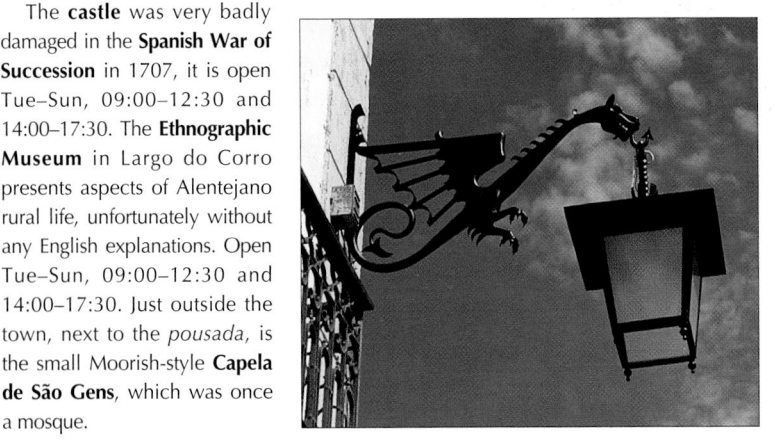

Beja
• Castle

• Serpa

Parque Natural do
Vale do Guadiana

Castle   Spain
★● Mértola

Mértola ★★

On the road from Serpa, just outside the village of **Mina
de São Domingo**, the Guadiana has been dammed to
form a lake. This would be a good place to stop for a
swim on one of the blisteringly hot days for which the
Alentejo is renowned; there are steps down to the
water, a picnic area and a diving board.

Situated at the highest navigable point of the
Guadiana, Mértola was visited by Phoenicians and
Carthaginians sailing upriver from the Algarve to trade.
The Romans called it **Mirtillis** and shipped wheat, wine
and olive oil (still staples of the local economy) south.
There are traces of the original quay on the **riverside**.
The **castle** dominates the town; the walls date from
Moorish times and include some original Roman
stonework. The keep was rebuilt in 1292 after the
Christian Reconquest. Open Tuesday–Sunday, 09:00–
12:30 and 14:00–17:30. Next to the castle is the
Mesquita, one of only two former mosques to survive
the Christian purge of Islam from Portugal. Inside are
12 Moorish columns supporting arabesque domes. The
mihrab, or prayer niche, faces east to Mecca.

The **Convento de São Francisco**, located on the
River Oeiras just to the southwest of Mértola, is owned
by a Dutch artist and is a combined nature reserve and
art gallery. Open daily 10:00–17:00.

Much of the surrounding countryside – comprising
moors, hills, woods and sheltered river valleys – lies
within the relatively new **Parque Natural do Vale do**

Right: *Mértola's castle
dominates the skyline.*

Guadiana. Among the abundant birdlife are storks (you'll see them nesting in town as well), kestrels, Bonelli's eagle and royal owl.

BEJA

This is the capital of the Baixa Alentejo and was an important Roman city and a centre of Moorish scholarship. But it was badly damaged in the Spanish and French wars and buildings of historical importance are few.

Nossa Senhora da Conceição Convent ★★★

Occupying the square of the same name, the Franciscan convent dates from the 15th century and was once one of the richest and most important in Portugal. The 17th-century high **altar** in the church is decadent, with bare-breasted sirens adding more than a touch of hothouse eroticism. The Baroque **processional** of **St John the Evangelist**, carried through town on the saint's feast day, is surmounted by a gold filigree crown and features a tableau of the saint about to be boiled in a cauldron, with two Moorish-looking figures lighting the fire.

In the barrel vault are some wonderful blue and yellow *azulejos,* while the cloister has Moorish tiles in a profusion of colours, abstract florals and geometric shapes. The museum upstairs contains local artefacts from Neolithic times onwards. The reconstruction of the terracotta **grille**, through which the errant nun (see panel) and her lover communed, will leave some visitors pondering whether or not the relationship was actually consummated. Open Tuesday–Sunday, 09:30–12:30 and 14:00–17:15.

Castle ★★★

Originally the outer wall of this Dom Dinis masterpiece from 1303 had 40 towers; now only a few remain. The view from the top of the 40m (131ft) **keep** is impressive. Look downwards at the metal grilles strategically placed for pouring boiling oil on attackers. Open Tuesday–Sunday, 10:00–13:00 and 14:00–18:00.

Above: *The cool cloisters of Beja's Convento da Nossa Senhora da Conceição.*

BEJA'S NAUGHTY NUN

Sister Mariana Alcoforado of the Convento da Nossa Senhora da Conceição had a secret love affair with a French officer who lived in Beja during the Spanish War of 1661–1668. The love letters she wrote to him after his departure were published in France as *Letters of a Portuguese Nun.* They scandalized Portuguese society but have since become one of the classics of romantic literature. In 1972 they inspired three Portuguese women writers and poets to publish *The New Portuguese Letters,* which highlighted the plight of women under the Salazar dictatorship.

Alentejo at a Glance

Spring (March to May) and **autumn** (late September to November) are probably the best times for a touring or active holiday; temperatures are pleasant and the risk of rain less than in the winter. **Summers** are very hot and you may find a swimming pool an asset. **Winter** nights are chilly but you should get your fair share of fine sunny days; pack some layers and rainwear just in case.

The transport hubs of the Alentejo are Évora for the north and Beja for the south. There are several daily express **bus** services from Lisbon to Évora taking around two hours; the less frequent **railway service** takes at least three. Beja is served by express coaches from both Lisbon and Faro, via Albufeira. If coming by **car**, new motorways have cut the time it takes to reach Évora from Lisbon to under two hours. If you're coming from the Algarve, the quickest route is to take the fast IP1 dual carriageway from just north of Albufeira. If you've got a bit more time on your hands, the road from São Bras de Alportel to Almodovar winds over the hills of the Serra do Caldeirão; if you're driving from the eastern Algarve the road from Vila Real to Mértola runs parallel to the Guadiana River.

A **car** is recommended as public transport (effectively buses and trains) is not that frequent. Having said that, from Beja buses connect with Serpa, Évora and Mértola. Estremoz and Vila Viçosa are served by **buses** from Évora; for Marvão and Castelo de Vide change at Portalegre, and for Monsaraz change at Reguengos.

Évora
LUXURY
Pousada Dos Lois, Largo Marquês de Marialva, tel: 266 730 070. Restored convent, opposite the Roman temple.

MID-RANGE
Residencial Solar Monfalim, Largo da Misericórdia, tel: 266 750 000. Comfortable, central property, previously an aristocrat's house.

BUDGET
Pensão Giraldo, Rua dos Mercadores 27, tel: 266 705 833. There are a dozen *quintas* (country manors which offer B&B) in the countryside around town; the tourist office can supply details and help with bookings.

Alvito
LUXURY
Pousada Castelo de Alvito, tel: 284 480 700, www.pousadas.pt Within the 15th-century castle; outdoor pool.

Estremoz
LUXURY
Pousada Rainha Santa Isabel, Largo de Dom Dinis, tel: 268 332 075, www.pousadas.pt Converted castle with antiques, overlooking town; has a pool.

MID-RANGE
Hospedaria Dom Dinis, Rua 31 de Janeiro 46, tel: 268 332 717. Good value in modern part of town.

BUDGET
Pensão Mateus, Rua do Almeida 39, tel: 268 322 226. Central location, friendly.

Vila Viçosa
LUXURY
Pousada de Dom João IV, tel: 268 980 742, www.pousadas.pt Former convent attached to duke's palace.

MID-RANGE
Casa de Pexinhos, tel: 268 980 472. Grand 17th-century manor.

Castelo de Vide
MID-RANGE
Hotel Sol e Serra, Estrada de S Vicente, tel: 245 900 000, www.grupofbarata.com Three-star; swimming pool.

Aldeia da Serra (near Redondo)
LUXURY
Hotel Convento de São Paulo, tel: 266 989 160, www.hotelconventospaulo.com

Former convent, pool, views over Serra d'Ossa.

Monsaraz
MID-RANGE
Horta da Moura, tel: 266 550 100, www.hortadamoura.pt In lovely valley, with pool, horses and bikes for hire.

Beja
LUXURY
Pousada de São Francisco, tel: 284 313 580, www.pousadas.pt Converted Franciscan monastery; pool.

All the *pousadas* listed above have fine (if expensive) restaurants offering regional dishes.

Évora
Restaurante Cozinha de Santo Humberto, Rua da Moeda 39, tel: 266 704 251. Regional specialities, popular.
Café Arcada, Praça do Giraldo 10. Bar/café, drinks, light meals.

Estremoz
Adega dos Isaias, Rua do Almeida 21, tel: 268 322 318. Lots of authentic local dishes in suitably rustic atmosphere.
Café Alentejano, Rossio 16, tel: 268 337 300. Local food.

Beja
Adega Tipica 25 Abril, Rua da Moeda. Rustic surroundings, good food, reasonable prices.

Bike Lab, Rua Fernando Seno 27, Évora, tel: 266 735 500. Bicycle hire.
Policarpo, Rua 5 de Outubro, Évora, tel: 266 746 970. City tours, minibus tours to megaliths and visits to nearby towns such as Vila Vicosa and Estremoz.
Turaventur, Rua João de Deus 21, Évora, tel/fax: 266 743 134. Biking, hiking, canoeing and jeep tours of the area for small groups (minimum six).
Mendes & Murteira, Rua 31 de Janeiro 15a, Évora, tel: 266 707 468, www.evora-mm.pt Tours of city and megalithic sites, also riding and jeep safaris.

General
Hotel Rura da Poupa, Rosmaninhal, Castelo Branco, tel: 277 470 000, www.monfortur.pt In the Tagus valley and unspoilt surroundings with plenty of wildlife and lots of outdoor activities.

Tourist Offices
Évora: Praça do Giraldo, tel: 266 730 030, www.cm-evora.pt/guiaturistico

Estremoz: Largo da Republica, tel: 268 333 541, www.cm-estremoz.pt
Portel: Camara Municipal, Largo D Nuno Alvares Pereira, tel: 266 619 030.
Monsaraz: Largo D Nuno Alvares Pereira, tel: 266 557 136.
Viana do Alentejo: Praça da República, tel: 266 953 106.
Vila Viçosa: Camara Municipal, tel: 268 881 101, www.cm-vilavicosa.pt
Castelo de Vide: Rua Bartolomeu Alvares de Santa 81–83, tel: 245 901 361, www.cm-castelo-vide.pt
Marvão: Largo de Santa Maria, tel: 245 993 886, www.cm-marvao.pt
Elvas: Praça da República, tel: 268 622 236, www.cm-elvas.pt
Beja: Rua Capitão João Francisco de Sousa, tel: 284 311 913, www.cm-beja.pt
Mértola: Rua Alonso Gomes 18, tel: 286 610 109, www.cm-mertola.pt
Serpa: Largo D. Jorge 2/3, tel: 284 544 727, www.cm-serpa.pt
Vila Nova de Milfontes: Rua Antonio Mantas, tel: 283 996 599.

ÉVORA	J	F	M	A	M	J	J	A	S	O	N	D
AVERAGE TEMP. °C	9	10	12	14	16	20	24	25	20	18	12	10
AVERAGE TEMP. °F	48	50	54	58	61	68	75	77	68	65	54	50
RAINFALL mm	81	71	96	56	46	8	5	3	38	58	76	79
RAINFALL ins.	3.2	2.8	3.8	2.2	1.8	0.3	0.2	0.1	1.5	2.3	3	3.1
DAYS OF RAINFALL	12	9	13	7	6	3	2	–	5	7	10	10

6
Oporto and the North

The north is probably the most traditional part of Portugal. In the tiny farms of the **Minho,** maize is stored in hand-built shelters, *espiguiros,* which have hardly altered since the days of the Celtic tribes. Long-horned **oxen** pull crude wooden carts and, in the chilly **mountains,** share the family home in order to generate warmth. Wolves and wild ponies roam the **Peneda-Gerês National Park,** and **folk tradition** is alive and well in rural communities, where the local **church** still has a degree of influence which has vanished in the more secular south.

By contrast, **Oporto** is the powerhouse of Portuguese industry; national and international companies have their headquarters here. Textiles, leather goods, electronics, wood products and wine are shipped from the mouth of the mighty **Douro** to all points of the compass. But it's precisely because it has a life of its own that Oporto appeals to visitors. You won't find shops full of tourist tat or restaurants serving bland versions of classic dishes here.

It is Oporto (or Porto as the Portuguese term it) which put the Port in Portugal when the nation was formed in the 11th century, and is also responsible for putting **port** onto the tables of a grateful world. Port wine grapes are grown in the **Douro valley,** and a tour upriver by boat will reveal one of the classic landscapes of Old Europe. Alternatively, head north to the Minho, an ancient province with equally strong wine traditions and miles of deserted sandy beaches. Or turn inland to **Trás-os-Montes,** the land 'behind the mountains', for a glimpse of some of the most isolated rural settlements in Europe.

DON'T MISS

*** Vale do Côa: go back in time to the Paleolithic in suitably wild scenery.
** Oporto: stroll around the old town and sample some fine port.
** Viana do Castelo: base yourself in this civilized and appealing little town.
** Douro Valley: explore by boat, rail or car.
** Peneda-Gerês and Montesinho Parks: hike or drive into the rewarding and remote northern mountains.

Opposite: *The mighty Douro River runs through the centre of Oporto.*

CLIMATE

Coastal areas of the north enjoy a typically mild Atlantic climate with no extremes of temperature and plenty of rain throughout the year; the driest months are June–August, and you can expect afternoon temperatures of 20°C (68°F) and more from May to October. It's a different story inland, where there is less rain but average summer temperatures are around 28°C (82°F) and can go much higher in the south-facing valleys of the Douro. Snow falls on the mountains in winter and frost is common.

Opposite: *A view of the Stock Exchange Palace in the heart of old Oporto.*
Below: *The lovely church of São Ildefonso, one of many fine examples to be found in Oporto.*

OPORTO

The lifeblood of Portugal's second city is the **Douro,** and the medieval **quayside** area, formerly dilapidated, was declared a UNESCO World Heritage Site in 1996. On the city side of the river the old **houses**, built into the cliff rising from the banks, are now being restored. Wander through the steep cobbled lanes and soak up the atmosphere; many old **wine warehouses** on the river's edge have been converted into smart restaurants and cafés. The most pleasant orientation is to take a Five Bridges **cruise** from here aboard a replica *barco rabelo*, the gaily painted shallow-keeled **ships** which once carried barrels of port downstream. These hour-long mini-cruises chug up and down the river and under the famous bridges; pick of the crop are the two elegant **metal bridges**, one designed by the famous French engineer Eiffel.

Cathedral ★

Just above the river the fortress-like cathedral has been considerably altered since it was built in the 12th century and much of the detail is Baroque. The silver **altarpiece** is a fine example; the 14th-century **cloisters** contain some outstanding *azulejos* depicting scenes from the life of the Virgin and Ovid's *Metamorphoses*. Open daily, 09:00–12:30 and 14:30–18:00.

Palácio da Bolsa ★★

A few hundred metres west of the cathedral, facing **Praça do Infante Dom Henrique**, is an outstanding monument to Oporto's other god – Mammon. The Palácio da Bolsa, formerly the **Stock Exchange**, was built between 1842 and 1910 and is currently the headquarters of the Oporto Commercial Association. It is regularly used for entertaining visiting heads of state. The **Hall of Nations**, formerly the dealing room, is a beautiful big square room with an atrium roof and the coats of arms of trading nations. Highlights of the upstairs rooms include the **Golden Room** with pre-Raphaelite paintings and a superb view of the city, and the sumptuous Moorish fantasy decor of the **Arabian Room**, inspired by Granada's Alhambra. Guided tours run approximately every half hour; open Monday–Friday, 09:00–13:00 and 14:00–18:00, plus weekends from April to October.

Igreja de São Francisco ★★

Next door, don't let the plain façade of this church put you off. Inside is a riot of **Baroque** decoration and carving, with **gold leaf** covering every surface. All this ostentatious display was too much for Oporto's rather austere clergy, and services have been discontinued. Open daily, 09:30–18:00; closed lunchtimes.

Port Houses ★★

A five-minute walk across the **Ponte Dom Luís I** leads you to the Port Houses on the opposite bank. Over 20 run tours; the tourist office on the riverfront next door to **Sandeman's Lodge** has details of which are open on the day. Monday–Saturday, 09:30–12:00 and 14:00–17:30, are the core times. In these fascinating tours you'll learn a great deal about the history and production of this great tipple – and sample some of the finished product.

OPORTO HISTORY

The name 'Portugal' derives from twin settlements on opposite banks of the mouth of the Douro, Portus and Cale, which gave their names to the ancient county of Portu-Cale – it was bounded by the Douro to the south and Minho River to the north. The building of the cathedral in 1111 enhanced Oporto's status, and Dom João I married Philippa of Lancaster here in 1337. Their famous son, Henry the Navigator, was born here; his birthplace is said to be Casa do Infante in Rua da Alfândega. Oporto has a long tradition of dissent and republicanism; the Inquisition was only briefly established here, and its citizens have rioted against taxes, arrested the French governor in 1808 and supported the liberal side in the War of the Two Brothers. The city was besieged by the absolutist Miguelite troops for three years but with the help of British troops fended them off.

Housed in an 18th-century manor near the university on Rua de Dom Manuel II, the **Museu Nacional Soares dos Reis** (open 10:00–18:00, closed Mon and Tue morning; free Sun a.m.) contains 17th- to 20th-century paintings, ceramics, glass and striking sculptures by Soares dos Reis. A new Museum of Contemporary Art (tel: 226 156 500; 10:00–19:00) has opened in the grounds of Casa de Serralves to the west of the city centre, just off Rua da Serralves. It is well worth a visit and features eclectic works from the 1960s onwards, including some Warhols and Rothkos as well as talented Portuguese artists. Casa de Serralves itself is a striking Art Deco mansion that is now used for exhibitions. The landscaped gardens surrounding both are lovely and make a nice picnic spot on a hot day. In summer they host al fresco jazz concerts.

In the centre of Oporto, **Praça do Liberdade** and **Praça do General Humberto Delgado** are twin squares forming a huge open space with the town hall at the north side. Walk west along **Rua dos Clérigos** for the best bird's-eye view of the city, available from the top of the **Torre dos Clérigos** (open daily, 10:30–12:00 and 14:00–17:00). This 240-step Baroque tower was designed by an Italian architect in the mid-18th century.

Hiring a **car** is not worth the effort in Oporto – heavy traffic, a maze of tiny lanes and lack of parking mean that walking, taxis, the brand new metro and buses are the easiest way to get around. If you want to take a ride to the **seaside** on one of Oporto's trams, pick it up at the **Tram Museum** on Alameda de Basílio Teles.

Even if you don't intend to take the train, take a look at the massive *azulejo* panels in **São Bento** train station, which depict both scenes from the city's history and everyday traditional life. For another *azulejo* hit, walk along **Rua de Santa Caterina** (a pedestrianized shopping street) to the **Capela das Almas**, where the entire façade is covered in cobalt blue and white *azulejos*. Nearby, drop into **Café Majestic** (Rua de Santa Caterina 112), a real old-fashioned coffee shop and something of an institution in Oporto. The romantic **Art Nouveau** decor includes jolly cherubs surrounding jovial busts of Jupiter and Ceres.

DOURO VALLEY

If time is short or if you don't have a car, the best way to get a feel for this striking valley, with its steep **terraced cliffs** covered in high-yield **vines**, is to take the train, which runs alongside some of the most scenic stretches of the river, or book an organized tour. In those lasting a day you cruise up the Douro and return by coach; two-day tours involve an overnight stay in one of the small hotels typical of the area, which were once wine magnates' country houses. You can also do a two-hour mini-cruise between **Peso da Régua** and **Pinhão**, the modern centres of quality port wine production.

Amarante ★★

This pleasant town, situated on the banks of the Tâmega River, was put on the map by **São (St) Gonçalo**. The 16th-century **monastery** and **church** (open daily 08:00–18:00) which bear his name feature an **arcade** containing statues of the kings who ruled around that time. Gonçalo is also the patron saint of marriage so single ladies may like to visit the saint's tomb and rub the hands or feet of the statue. They will be married within the year according to local tradition.

FRENCH FAREWELL

In 1809 the French were in retreat from Portugal, having been driven out of Oporto by Sir Arthur Wellesley, the Duke of Wellington. Looting and burning as they went, a detachment arrived at Amarante where they were held at bay by Portuguese troops and local volunteers long enough to allow towns-folk to escape. In revenge, the French burned much of the town to the ground. You can still see the burned-out skeleton of an old manor house, **Casa de Calçada**, near the railway station.

Opposite: *These old-fashioned boats used to transport barrels of wine from the Upper Douro to the riverfront wine lodges.*

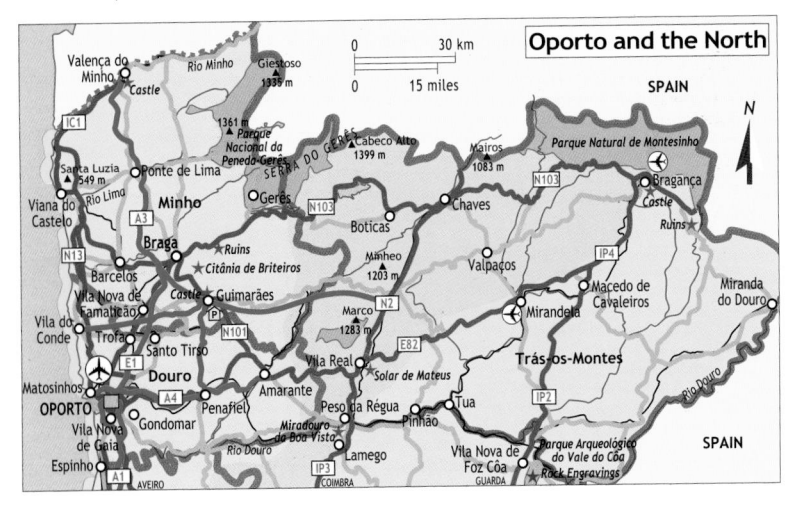

PORT

Douro wines did not travel well on the long and often rough sea crossing to England so local merchants came up with the inspired idea of adding brandy to stabilize the wine. The effects were to increase the sweetness and alcohol content and arrest fermentation so the wine could be stored for longer. By the 18th century, port was so popular that English companies such as Taylor's and Croft's were well established in Oporto. In 1756 the Marquês de Pombal founded a state monopoly to control quality and prices, and specified that only wines from a single region in the Alto Douro could be used in port. So the Douro became the world's first demarcated wine region. The cheapest ports are ruby and young tawnies; vintage port is rare, sublime and expensive. Try a late-bottled vintage for high quality at a reasonable price. White port, served chilled with a slice of lemon, makes a nice aperitif.

Amid all the sombre granite Romanesque churches which characterize Amarante is a bright little **art gallery** (next to the tourist office) which features the work of **Amadeo de Souza Cardosa**, who studied under Cézanne and developed his own version of Impressionism. In the attached **museum**, look out for the twin statues of black devils with horns and negroid features. These are copies of the original and very old statues associated with pagan rites, which were burnt by the invading French troops. The statues outraged one Bishop of Braga and he had their prominent sexual organs removed.

Solar de Mateus ★★

Vila Real is a busy commercial town with little to attract the visitor, although it makes a good base for exploring the surrounding mountains. But 4km (2.5 miles) to the east is one of the most familiar images of Portugal. The fairytale Baroque façade of the 18th-century **Mateus Palace** appears on the labels of Mateus Rosé, at one time one of the most popular wine brands in the world. Designed by Nicolau Nasoni, who was also responsible for Oporto's Torre dos Clérigos, the soaring spires and squiggles of this romantic creation are mirrored in the waters of an ornamental lake. Open daily, 09:00–13:00 and 14:00–18:00.

Lamego ★★

This small town with a strong **religious tradition** is famous for its delicious **sparkling wine** (Raposeira is the brand) and **smoked ham**. The **cathedral** is one of the oldest in Portugal and dates from the 12th century although it has been extensively rebuilt since then – the interior was

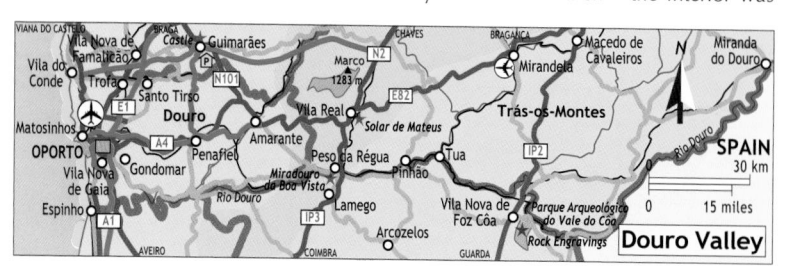

refurbished in the 18th century. The nearby **museum**, housed in the former 18th-century episcopal palace, mostly concentrates on religious art.

Lamego's main claim to fame is the Baroque 18th-century church, **Igreja de Nossa Senhora dos Remédios** (Our Lady of the Cures). Inside it's a pleasant church with a Baroque altar, blue and yellow *azulejos* and stained-glass windows depicting scenes from the life of the Virgin. Outside is a lovely **terrace** full of fountains, palm trees and statues representing David, Solomon and other kings of Judah; a ceremonial stairway leads up from town. Devotees of the Virgin climb up here on their knees in the annual religious **festival**, which lasts for three weeks from the end of August to the beginning of September. It's the biggest pilgrimage in Portugal after Fátima (*see* page 56).

Above: *Enthusiastic guides at Foz Côa Archaeological Park help recreate the past.*

Foz Côa Archaeological Park ★★★

Now a UNESCO World Heritage Site, these fantastic Palaeolithic **rock engravings**, discovered in 1992 during a survey for a proposed hydroelectric dam which would have flooded the valley, have now been saved for posterity. Mating horses, giant aurochs, wild goats and salmon figure prominently and have been drawn beautifully. They are engraved on exposed rock faces, not cave walls, amid breathtakingly wild scenery. At least 10,000 years separates the earliest engravings from the latest and it's the biggest known site of open-air Palaeolithic art in the world. Allow a day and a half to visit the three main sites; access is by the park's 4WD vehicles. One site involves a 90-minute walk; it's great walking country but bear in mind that summer temperatures can top 40°C (104°F). Open year-round; booking essential – *see* page 109 for details. Try also to visit the excellent **Ervamoira Museum**, located in a remote *quinta* belong to port producers Ramos Quinta, for an overview of the area's history and natural history.

LOCAL DELICACIES

The north of Portugal specializes in hearty dishes which are high in calories to keep out the winter chill. Soups include *canja de galinha* (chicken broth), *feijão frade* (black-eyed bean soup) and *caldo de castanhas* (chestnut soup). *Broa de milho* (corn bread) makes a tasty accompaniment. *Dobrada* (tripe stew) is not to everyone's taste but is much savoured by Oporto's gourmets, as is *chispe* (pig's trotter with white beans). *Carne asado* (slow-roasted pork or lamb with potatoes in a clay pot) is another favourite, as is *rancho* (macaroni stew with chick peas, sausage, bacon and beef). *Presunto* (air-dried ham), *chouriço* (sausage) and *queso da serra* (fresh mountain cheese) are all produced locally and are quite delicious.

NORTHERN DANCERS

Trás-os-Montes has a rich tradition of folk dances, many of which appear to date back to pre-Christian agricultural and fertility rituals. In the Chaves area the climax of a dance performed at the winter solstice is the entry of a wild man of the woods, masked and wearing a fox tail, who dances suggestively with the girls. Other dances centre around courtship, and the highlight of one farmers' dance is men rushing at each other and bouncing off their bellies. The costumes are old-fashioned work clothes and the musical instruments are Celtic pipes and drums. In Miranda del Douro Pauliteiros, men dressed in white skirts, with waistcoats, shawls and black hats covered in ribbons, clack their sticks together in a spirited and ancient dance very similar to the English Morris tradition. You'll definitely catch them performing in their home town in the third weekend of August; otherwise look out for guest appearances at other festivals around Portugal.

TRÁS-OS-MONTES

If you don't have a car, one of the best ways to get to this remote area is by rail from Oporto, changing at **Tua** on the Douro to the narrow-gauge line which leads you through beautiful scenery to **Mirandela**, from where there are plenty of bus connections. Winding country lanes reveal a bleak landscape on the mountain ridges, full of gorse bushes and granite outcrops. In the more sheltered valleys tiny farming settlements are surrounded by woods and fast-flowing trout streams.

Chaves ★★

The name means 'keys' and, as the gateway to northern Portugal, this spa town has been fought over by Romans, Visigoths, Moors, Spaniards and French. Start by the river, noting the **Roman bridge**. Then head towards the **old town**, glancing upwards at the traditional **balconies** made of wrought iron and wood. In the main square is a statue of **Dom Afonso** (1371–1461), the first Duke of Bragança and defender of Chaves. The keep is all that remains of his castle home and it contains a **military museum**. The 17th-century **Igreja da Misericórdia** features a Baroque gold altar, *azulejo*-tiled interior and a frescoed ceiling. The **regional museum**, with plenty of Roman finds, is open 09:00–12:00 and 14:00–17:30 daily.

Bragança ★★★

This once isolated town has Celtic roots and gave its name to a royal dynasty. Stroll around the medieval old town; you'll see the oldest **town hall** in Portugal, dating from the 12th century, and an ancient **Iron-Age pig**, sculpted from granite, upon which rests the town's pillory. **The Museu do Abade de Baçal**, on Rua Abilio Beca, is worth a visit for its insights into regional history and architecture. Open daily 10:00–17:00, except Monday. Bragança is a good base for exploring the **Montesinho Natural Park**, whose oak and chestnut forests and high moors extend into Spain.

THE MINHO

This ancient province provides plenty of contrast, from historic towns such as **Guimarães**, the first capital, to the long sandy beaches of the coast and Portugal's only national park, **Peneda-Gerês,** in the mountains on the Spanish border. In between is a distinctive **rural** landscape, surprisingly highly populated in the fertile south and west, but the foothills of the mountains contain tiny villages which still operate a pre-medieval barter system and rely on oxen for heavy farm work.

There are few heavyweight historic sights here; the real pleasures of a holiday in the Minho are lifestyle-based, exploring the pretty countryside or relaxing in a beautiful old garden, glass of *vinho verde* in hand.

Guimarães ★★

The medieval old town is located to the northeast of the modern city. The sturdy **seven-towered castle** (open daily 09:30–17:00) was built around 1100. Nearby, the 15th-century **Paço dos Duques** (open daily 09:00–17:30) was, in its time, the most lavish palace in the whole

> **THE BEST BEDS**
>
> If you want to hobnob with the cream of the Portuguese aristocracy this is the place, as dozens of pedigreed families in the region have thrown open the doors of their stately homes to overnight guests. For the same price as a hotel you'll get a much more interesting experience, plus lots of local knowledge.

Opposite: *Traditional dancers and musicians in Chaves await their cue.*
Below: *Casa de Juste in the Minho is one of many old mansions where visitors can stay.*

Iberian Peninsula. On display are tapestries, old carpets, antique furniture, weapons and armoury. The cloisters of the **Convento de Nossa Senhora de Oliveira** contain the **Museu Alberto Sampaio** (open daily, 07:00–12:00 and 15:30–19:30, except Monday), which has an interesting collection of *azulejos*, ceramics and religious artefacts. The **Museu Martins Sarmento** contains fascinating pieces excavated from local Celtic sites. Open daily except Monday, 10:00–12:00 and 14:00–17:00.

Braga ★

The capital of both the Minho region and the Christian faith in Portugal, this town was where the powerful arch-bishops, known as the **Primates of Portugal,** exercised their considerable (secular as well as spiritual) power for 700 years from the 11th century onwards. There are at least three dozen **churches** in the city and the tourist office has all the details. Pride of place must go to the **Sé** (cathedral) which is a mixture of Romanesque, Gothic and Baroque architecture, having been extensively added to over the centuries. Outside, the Manueline **pinnacles** and the **statue** of the nursing Virgin are noteworthy; inside are various Gothic **chapels** and a treasury stuffed full of gold, silver and jew-elled priestly accessories.

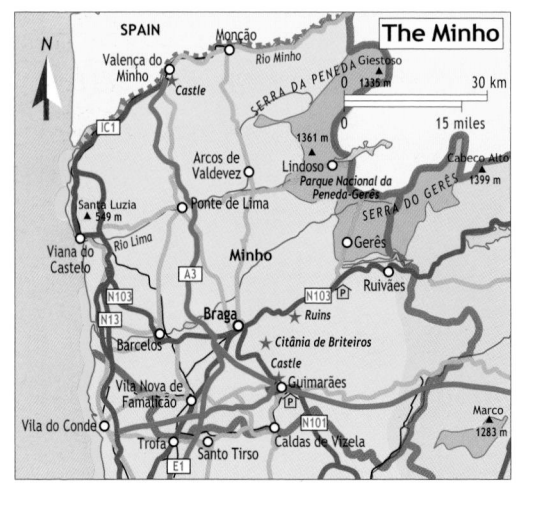

Some 12km (7.5 miles) to the south of Braga is the **Citânia de Briteiros,** the excavated remains of a **Celtic hill settlement**. The remains, which are over 2500 years old, include a bath house and the foundations of stone cottages. Some of the finds from the site are displayed in the Museu Martins Sarmento in Guimarães. Open daily 09:00–17:30.

Some of the loveliest countryside in the Minho lies along the **Lima valley** and there is a particularly wide choice of rural guest-houses, ranging from farm-houses to counts' mansions, in the area around the sleepy market town of Ponte de Lima. Follow the Lima upstream and you'll arrive in the **Peneda-Gerês National Park**, with its wild scenery, remote villages and excellent hiking.

Viana do Castelo ★★

This is perhaps the most appealing town in the northern Minho. There's good **swimming** and **windsurfing** to be had from the nearby beaches to the north and south. Wine exports, cod-fishing and trade with Brazil made Viana prosperous and there are many fine buildings around town, particularly around **Praça da República**. At the centre of the square is a handsome Renaissance **fountain**; the **town hall** dates from the same period. Next door is the striking Misericórdia **alms house** dating from 1589, its Venetian influence showing through an arched colonnade with loggias supported on caryatids. The attached **church** (open on Sunday morning) has some lovely *azulejos*. Just south of the square the parish church has a fine Gothic doorway.

To the north of town is a steep hill, **Monte de Santa Luzia**, topped by a modern basilica, a *pousada* and a partially excavated Celtic village. The **view** is absolutely spectacular; walk up through the pine woods or take a taxi. Viana hosts a lively traditional **festival** over the third weekend in August; although dedicated to the Virgin of Sorrows and featuring solemn processions, there is also plenty of dancing, drinking and fireworks.

Above: *The River Lima winds down to the Atlantic at Viana do Castelo.*

RIVER OF FORGETFULNESS

It was just a slow-running river meandering through straggly vineyards, but something about the Lima spooked the battle-hardened Roman legionaries on their route march to conquer Hispania Ulterior around 60BC. They decided it was the Lethe and refused to cross, fearing that the fabled waters of oblivion would erase all memories of their distant home. Their leader, the consul Decimus Brutus, plunged in and crossed to the other side, where he shouted out the names of his men one by one. Thus encouraged, the legion crossed and continued their progress north.

Oporto and the North at a Glance

If you don't mind rain, **spring** is lovely when the flowers are in bloom. **Summer** has the most reliable weather and is rarely too hot. **Autumn** can be changeable; there are many rural festivities after the grape harvest (late September). **Winters** are damp and snowy in the mountains but bars and restaurants are welcoming and you'll avoid the crowds.

Oporto has **direct flights** from several European capitals and a frequent **shuttle service** from Lisbon. It's a day's drive from the capital, with frequent **train** and **bus** services also an option. Coach and rail links exist via northern Spain. If **driving** from Spain, you can use the many minor roads that cross the border; main access points on fast roads are at or near Valença, Chaves and Bragança.

Regional **trains** from Oporto go north to Viana do Castelo and the Spanish border and east to the upper Douro valley, Amarante and Mirandela. The major towns are linked by **bus** services operated by different companies and leaving from different locations; if you don't speak Portuguese, a tourist office is your best source of information. If **driving**, note that distances may look short on the map but the journey on narrow and winding roads

may take much longer. Go slowly, enjoy the view and look out for animals on the road.

Associação de Turismo de Habitação (Turihab):
Association of owner-managed guesthouses and self-catering cottages on country estates and farms; categories include *Solares de Portugal* (luxurious manor houses); *Quintas* (farms and manor houses) and *Casas Rusticas* (simpler farmhouses). **Turihab**, Praça da República, 4990 Ponte de Lima, tel: 258 742 827, www.turihab.pt

Oporto
LUXURY
Hotel Infante de Sagres, Praça Dona Filipa de Lencastre 62, tel: 223 39 8500, www.hotelinfantesagres.pt. Excellent, sumptuous rooms with antiques.
Mercure Batalha, Praça da Batalha 116, tel: 222 043 300. Central.

MID-RANGE
Pao de Açucar, Rua do Almada 262, tel: 222 00 2425, www. residencialpaodeacucar.com
Residencial Vera Cruz, Rua de Ramalho Ortigao 14, tel: 223 323 396.

BUDGET
Pensão Astoria, Rua Arnaldo Gama 56, tel: 222 008 175. Great views of the river from some rooms in this simple but friendly establishment.

Douro Valley
LUXURY
Pousada de São Gonçalo, 4600 Amarante, tel: 255 460 030, www.pousadas.pt In Marão mountains.
Vintage House, Lugar da Ponte, 5085 Pinhão, tel: 254 730 230, www.hotelvintage house.com Former port estate manor, beautifully renovated.

MID-RANGE
Albergaria Dona Margaritta, Rua Candido dos Reis 53, Amarante, tel: 255 432 110, www.albergariadona margaritta.pa-net.pt
Hotel Parque, Parque de Nossa Senhora dos Remédios, Lamego, tel: 254 609 140, www. hotel-parque.com Set in park.

Trás-os-Montes
LUXURY
Forte de São Francisco Hotel, Chaves 5400, tel: 276 333 700, www.forte-s-francisco-hoteis.pt Within an old fort.
Pousada de São Bartolomeu, Bragança, tel: 273 331 493, www.pousadas.pt Just outside town, with pool.

MID-RANGE
Residencial Florinda, Rua dos Açougues, Chaves, tel: 276 333 392, fax: 276 326 577.
Residencial Tulipa, Rua Dr Francisco Felgueiras 8, Bragança, tel: 273 331 675.

Minho
LUXURY
Pousada de Santa Marinha,

Guimarães, tel: 253 511 249.
In a 17th-century monastery.
Pousada do Monte de Santa Luzia, Viana do Castelo, tel: 258 800 370, www.pousadas.pt

MID-RANGE

Paço de Calheiros, Ponte de Lima, tel: 258 947 164, www.solaresdeportugal.pt In 17th-century manor, pool, resident Count.
Residencial Magalhaes, Rua Manuel Espregueira 62, Viana do Castelo, tel 258 823 293. Central but in a quiet location, old fashioned, good value.

Adega Faustinho, Travessa do Olival, Chaves, tel: 276 322 142. Try the local wines.
Fiha de Mae Preta, Cais da Ribeira 40, Oporto, tel: 222 055 515. Under the arches next to the river, this long-established favourite serves local specialities.
Don Tonho, Cais da Ribeira 13–15, Oporto, tel: 222 004 307. Trendy establishment overlooking the river, serving traditional cuisine with a modern twist.
Os Tres Potes, Beco dos Fornos 7, Viana do Castelo, tel: 258 829 928. Very good; folk dancing on weekends.
Solar do Vinho do Porto, Quinta da Maceirinha, Rua de Entre Quintas, Oporto, tel: 226 094 749. Smart bar with waiter service and *the* place in town to sample some vintage port.

Naturimont-Sport Adventure, Rua Nova 26, 5100 Lamego, tel: 969 081 507, www.naturimont.com
Porto Tours, Torre Medieval, Calçada Pedro Pitoes 15, Oporto, tel: 222 000 073, www.portotours.com Run by the city council and the tourist office, this is a one stop shop for all the local tour operators – Douro cruises, city walking tours, scenic rail trips, soft adventure and the rest. They answer questions, give advice and make bookings. In Oporto, the leading companies offering Douro cruises and rail trips are **Barcadouro**, tel: 223 722 415, www.barcadouro.com **Endouro Turismo**, tel: 226 099 302, www.endouroturismo.pt and **Rota do Douro**, tel: 223 759 042, www.rottadodouro.com
Diver Lanhoso, Povoa de Lanhoso, tel: 253 635 763, www.diverlanhoso.pt Climbing, mountain biking and other outdoor pursuits in the Peneda-Geres National Park.

Tourist Offices
Oporto: Rua Clube dos Fenianos 25, tel: 223 39 3470.
Amarante: Alameda Teixeira de Pascoaes, tel: 255 420 246.
Lamego: Avenida Visconde Guedes Teixera, tel: 254 612 005.
Vila Real: Avenida Carvalho Araujo 94, tel: 259 322 819.
Chaves: Terreiro do Cavalaria, tel: 276 340 661.
Bragança: Avenida Cidade de Zamora, tel: 273 381 273,
Braga: Praça da República, tel: 253 262 550.
Guimarães: Alameda de Sao Damaso, tel: 253 412 450.
Viana do Castelo: Rua do Hospital Velho, tel: 258 822 620.
Parque Arqueológico Vale do Côa, Avenida Gago Coutinho 19, Vila Nova de Foz Côa, tel: 279 768 260, www.ipa.min-cultura.pt/pavc
Parque Natural de Montesinho, Rua Conego Albano Falcáo 5, Bragança, tel: 273 381 234, www.icn.pt
Parque Nacional da Peneda-Gerês, Quinta das Parretas, Avenida Antonio Macedo, Braga, tel: 253 203 480.

OPORTO	J	F	M	A	M	J	J	A	S	O	N	D
AVERAGE TEMP. °C	9	10	12	14	15	18	20	20	19	16	12	11
AVERAGE TEMP. °F	48	50	54	57	59	65	69	68	66	60	54	51
HOURS OF SUN DAILY	5	6	6	8	9	10	11	10	8	6	5	4
RAINFALL mm	159	112	147	86	86	41	20	26	51	105	148	168
RAINFALL ins.	6.3	4.4	5.8	3.4	3.4	1.6	0.8	1	2	4.1	5.8	6.6
DAYS OF RAINFALL	18	15	17	13	13	7	5	6	10	15	18	18

7. The Islands: Madeira and the Azores

These fascinating islands have more to offer than their physical presence as tiny dots on the map suggests. Both **Madeira** and the **Azores** archipelago are as Portuguese as anywhere on the mainland. They were the first unknown and uninhabited lands to be discovered by Henry the Navigator's ships in the early 15th century.

Madeira has a long pedigree as a holiday island. It was a vital port of call for British ships en route to the colonies in Africa and India, and in the 19th century the island's balmy climate made it a sought-after destination in which to escape the rigours of a British winter. **Funchal**, the island's capital, is packed full of four- and five-star hotels but the lush and **mountainous interior** is popular with walkers and mountain bikers; two top-class **golf courses** add to its enduring year-round popularity. There are few **beaches** on the rocky coast but swimmers can enter the water by ladders; by contrast, the neighbouring island of **Porto Santo** has a magnificent stretch of sand which makes it a family favourite.

The nine volcanic islands of the Azores, far out in the Atlantic, have an end-of-the-world appeal. Myth-makers would have us believe that they were once part of the great continent of **Atlantis**. Visitors come here to relax away from commercial pressures and to explore the green and mountainous **interior** or watch the magnificent **whales** which were once the mainstay of the islands' economy; now whaling has been banned, they are flourishing again in the deep offshore waters. Hiking, riding, golf and swimming with dolphins are other popular activities.

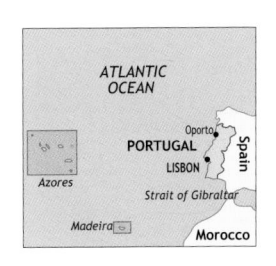

ATLANTIC OCEAN

Oporto

PORTUGAL

Spain

LISBON

Azores

Strait of Gibraltar

Madeira

Morocco

DON'T MISS

★★★ Savour the **end-of-the-world** feeling in the remote Azores islands.
★★★ Thrill to the sight of a massive **whale** surfacing just yards from your boat.
★★ Admire the **flowers** and shrubs of Funchal's botanical gardens.
★★ Enjoy a glass of fine old Madeira in an ancient **wine cellar**.
★★ Head for the hills along a **levada**.

Opposite: *Traditional Madeiran A-frame thatched house at Santana.*

Above: *The Botanical Gardens overlooking Funchal are a lovely place for a stroll.*

MADEIRA

Madeira condenses a great deal of scenery into a small frame. Just 57km (35 miles) by 23km (14 miles), it encompasses some spectacular terrain. The exotic landscape evokes the tropics – **Africa** amid the palms and terraced banana plantations of the coast, **Himalayan** subtropical forests inland, and **Mauritius** when you gaze through waving sugar cane to the volcanic peaks which soar to 1755m (5758ft) above sea level.

Over the centuries Portuguese settlers brought back hundreds of species of **flowers**, **shrubs** and **trees** from the tropics and these thrive in Madeira's mild climate alongside the island's native flora. Orchids, jacarandas, bougainvillea, lilies, hydrangeas, magnolias, and azaleas bloom effortlessly throughout the year and delight the eye at every turn.

Funchal ★★

Funchal is home to almost half the island's population of around 300,000. It is a bustling town with some elegant historical buildings, a **harbour** where cruise ships berth, a yacht **marina** and dozens of hotels. The **morning market** sells fruit piled high in wicker baskets, fresh fish and beautiful, colourful flowers.

The **municipal museum** (open Tuesday–Sunday, 10:00–18:00) is devoted to natural history and features a well-stocked aquarium. There are a number of **churches** worth a visit. Rich merchants donated fine paintings to the island's churches and the best of these can be seen in the **Museum of Sacred Art** (open Tuesday–Saturday, 10:00–12:30 and 14:30–18:00). Housed in a former episcopal palace with a beautiful arcaded gallery, it overlooks **Praça do Município**. On the other side of the square the 17th-century **Igreja do Colegio** has an extravagant Baroque altar and some fine *azulejos*. The 15th-century **cathedral** (the first to be built overseas) has a remarkable cedarwood ceiling inlaid with silver in the Moorish style.

No visit to Funchal would be complete without a tour of the oldest working wine cellars in Madeira, the **São Francisco Adega do Vinho** (St Francis Wine Lodge). The building, once a Franciscan monastery, dates from the 16th century. It is the home of the Madeira Wine Company, which incorporates many famous brand names. **Guided tours** take place twice daily and include a film relating the fascinating history of wine production in Madeira, a visit to the museum which houses documents and tools from the past, and a demonstration of the craft of cooperage. At the end of the tour, by which time appetites have been thoroughly whetted, there is the opportunity to sample some fine vintages.

Public Gardens ★★★

Among the many public gardens over-looking Funchal, perhaps the loveliest are the **Botanical Gardens**, **Quinta do Palheiro** and **Monte Palácio**. After a visit to the latter you can take an exciting toboggan ride back down to town. The traditional wicker toboggans, guided by men wearing straw hats and baggy white suits, were once used for transporting fruit and vegetables from the hill plantations down to market.

Below: *Hang onto your seats for a thrilling toboggan ride back to town.*

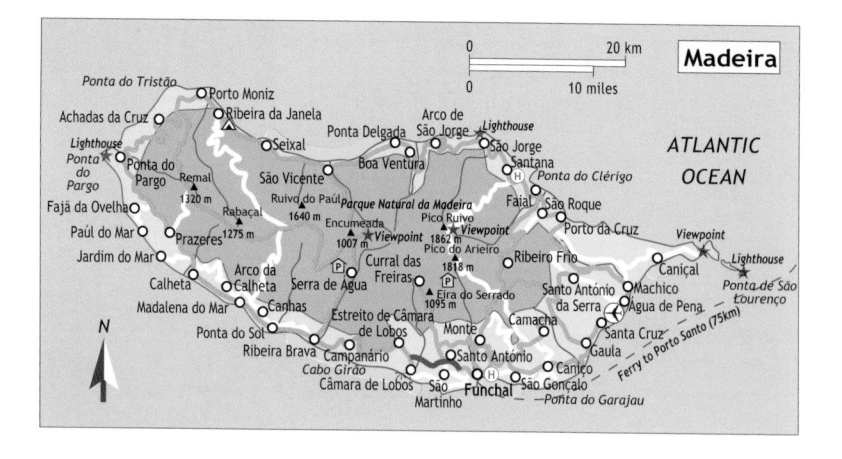

CURRAL DAS FREIRAS

Curral das Freiras is the only village in Madeira without a sea view and is best reached on foot along the island's famous mountain paths. The village is located at the bottom of a huge volcanic crater and was where, in the 16th century, the nuns of Funchal's Santa Clara convent hid from pirates.

Another hill village within easy reach of Funchal is **Camacha**, the centre of the Madeiran wickerwork industry. Here you can watch baskets and furniture being made in the traditional manner.

Fishing Villages ★

West of Funchal, the first fishing village you come to is the picturesque **Camara de Lobos**. Named after the sea lions which used to bask on the rocks, it's a favourite spot for artists who draw inspiration from the beautiful views. Beyond is **Cabo Girão**, the second tallest sea cliff in the world, which plunges almost 600m (1969ft) straight down to the Atlantic.

All Madeira's **fishing villages** have their charms, with narrow cobbled streets, old ochre-coloured houses with green shutters, and a fleet of brightly painted boats bobbing in the harbour. If you're touring in summer, you should pack a swimming costume for a dip in the natural rock pools on the north coast at **Porto Moniz**. The coast road between **Seixal** and **São Vicente** is spectacular and features no fewer than seven waterfalls which cascade down the cliffs onto the road.

The Mountains ★★★

Don't miss the high plateau of **Paul do Serra**, an aspect of Madeira which never fails to amaze. Here, over 1000m (3210ft) above sea level, the eerie and often misty landscape is reminiscent of Scottish moorland, except that the ground cover is bracken rather than heather. Windmills turn soundlessly, converting the Atlantic winds into electricity.

Further east lie the high peaks of **Pico Ruivo** and **Pico do Arieiro**. The former can only be reached by keen walkers, and the latter via a switchback road.

SPORTS AND ACTIVITIES

Madeira's climate makes it an ideal year-round destination for **outdoor activities**. Winters are mild, while summers are free from searing heat. There are two championship golf courses. **Santo da Serra** is set in eucalyptus forests almost 900m (2953ft) above sea level and offers spectacular views and plenty of challenges over the ravines and slopes. **Palheiro Golf** is beautifully landscaped around a 200-year-old country estate whose exotic trees and shrubs have been retained. Funchal's top five-star hotels offer guests a courtesy shuttle to the courses and reduced green fees.

Madeira is a paradise for **walkers**, who can expect magnificent views and the exotic vegetation of the tropics without the attendant heat, humidity and biting insects. There are many well-signposted trails in the mountains, while hikers who do not want to commit themselves to testing gradients can follow the *levadas* – watercourses which crisscross the island and irrigate plantations and market gardens. If you are not an energetic walker but would still like to explore the interior, try **horse riding** or **mountain biking** as alternative options.

Above: *Enthusiastic walkers can access Madeira's mountainous interior.*

Opposite: *Madeira's deep offshore waters teem with fish.*

LEVADAS

Early colonists were not slow to spot the potential of channelling Madeira's many underwater springs and reservoirs to the drier areas of the south coast. Today there is a network of over 2000km (1242 miles) of *levadas* crisscrossing the island. These aqueducts follow the contour lines and occasionally cling to rock faces over vertiginous drops; they were constructed by workmen suspended in wicker baskets. The maintenance paths which run alongside the *levadas* give walkers easy access into the interior to admire the scenery.

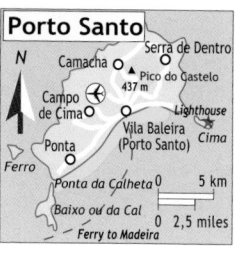

Porto Santo

Right: *Stallholders take a break from business for a hand of cards.*
Opposite: *Both familiar and unfamiliar varieties of fruit are found in the market.*

Water sports on offer include skiing, windsurfing, snorkelling, scuba diving and dinghy sailing. Madeira is gaining a growing reputation as a top-class game fishing destination, with blue marlin weighing over 450kg (992 lb) the main quarry; yellowfin tuna, swordfish and varieties of shark are also plentiful.

Nightlife is on the quiet side; however, high rollers can head for Funchal's **casino** where they can try their luck on the blackjack, roulette and chemin de fer tables, or on the slot machines. The neighbouring **Casino Park Hotel** lays on nightly international cabaret extravaganzas.

PORTO SANTO

Madeira's sister island can be reached by air or boat. **Beach lovers** are in their element here as the island features a 6km (4-mile) stretch of golden sand. The tranquil little island is a favourite summer retreat for Madeirans; there's little to see aside from an old house once occupied by the explorer, **Christopher Colombus**, when he married a local girl and a clutch of **churches** in the sleepy little capital, **Vila Baleira**.

Visitors to Porto Santo come to laze on the beautiful sandy beaches, eat the freshest of fresh seafood and enjoy the many water sports on offer. There's a riding centre, bikes to hire, and walking is also a pleasant way to explore the island.

DINING OUT

Eating well is one of the pleasures of a Madeiran holiday. Visit any market and you will see tropical fruits such as bananas, pineapples, mangoes, avocados and melons alongside apples, oranges and grapes. Atlantic-fresh seafood another treat, and a local speciality is the eel-shaped *espada* (scabbard fish) which can be fried, grilled or stewed. One of the most typical dishes in Madeira is *espetada* – beef cooked on a laurel wood skewer over an open fire. It's best eaten in the open air with hunks of home-made bread and plenty of light red wine.

The Azores

Nine tiny islands dotted like emerald gems in the wide Atlantic 1600km (994 miles) west of Lisbon, the Azores appeal to those who love beautiful **scenery** and prefer slow-paced holidays without the hustle and bustle of city life. The Portuguese name, Açores, is derived from *açor*, or goshawk, the bird which is featured on the islands' flag, surrounded by nine stars.

The **volcanoes** which characterize the archipelago are still active today – a severe earthquake destroyed two-thirds of the buildings on Faial in July 1999. The islands are an important migratory route for **whales,** and whale hunting was once the prime economic activity here. Many islanders have themselves migrated to the USA and in summer large numbers of Portuguese Americans return to visit their relations.

São Miguel ★★★

Saõ Miguel is the largest of the islands and is home to half the total population. It also receives the lion's share of tourists by virtue of its direct flights from Lisbon, beautiful countryside, lovely beaches and outstanding volcanic scenery.

Ponta Delgada is the islands' largest town and is also the seat of the autonomous regional government and the university. The old town contains an elegant Baroque **town hall,** some rather impressive 17th- and 18th-century **mansions**, and also a number of charming small **churches**.

Sete Cidades, 80km (50 miles) to the west, is the Azores' trademark beauty spot – a vast caldera (a flooded volcanic crater) surrounded by banks of **hydrangeas**. It is thought to have formed as recently as 1440 when a massive

ASKING THE WAY

If you do lose your way in the countryside you may have to ask directions from a local, and many older country folk don't speak English. Even if you have memorized the question in Portuguese it is not always easy to understand the answer. So keep it simple and ask questions which require a simple yes/no answer.
• Excuse me sir/madam: *Faz o favor senhor/senhora*
• To get to xx? *Para ir a xx?*
• Is it to the left/right/straight ahead? *É a esquerda/ a direita/sempre en frente?*
And don't forget to say thank you: *muito obrigado* (*obrigada* if you're female).

WHALING IN THE AZORES

The hunting of the sperm whale, the largest predator in the world, was first organized in the Azores by English whalers, although by the 18th century, American ships dominated the industry. Azorean seamen were known throughout the world for their daring, and harpooned their massive quarry from light rowing boats. Today the *vigias* or lookout towers on the coast are used by sightseeing boats to spot schools of whales; Faial and Pico are the main centres for whale watching and May to September is the best time to view these wonderful animals. As well as sperm whales, killer whales, bottlenose whales, pilot whales and dolphins are regularly seen in the offshore waters.

volcanic eruption demolished the existing peak. There are two **lakes** in the crater – one green and one blue – separated by a narrow neck of land.

In the east of the island **Achada das Furnas** is an area of geyser and hot spring activity in beautiful mountain surroundings. You can bathe in warm water at the pool in the lovely botanical gardens of **Parque Terra Nostra**, or head down to the coast at **Ribiera Quente** where the sea is warmed by underwater hot springs. The entire **eastern coast** is strikingly beautiful. In the centre of the island, **Lagoa do Fogo** is a lovely crater lake.

Santa Maria ★★

This small island is the most southerly in the archipelago and enjoys a relatively warm and sunny climate. It also has some good sandy beaches. It was settled by **farmers** from the **Algarve,** and the distinctive architecture of the white houses dotted throughout the countryside, each with a tall ornamental chimney, is very similar to that of the mainland province.

Terceira ★★★

As the name suggests, this is the third largest island in the Azores and was also the third to be discovered, Santa Maria and São Miguel being the first two. Emigrants from the Algarve and Alentejo settled here.

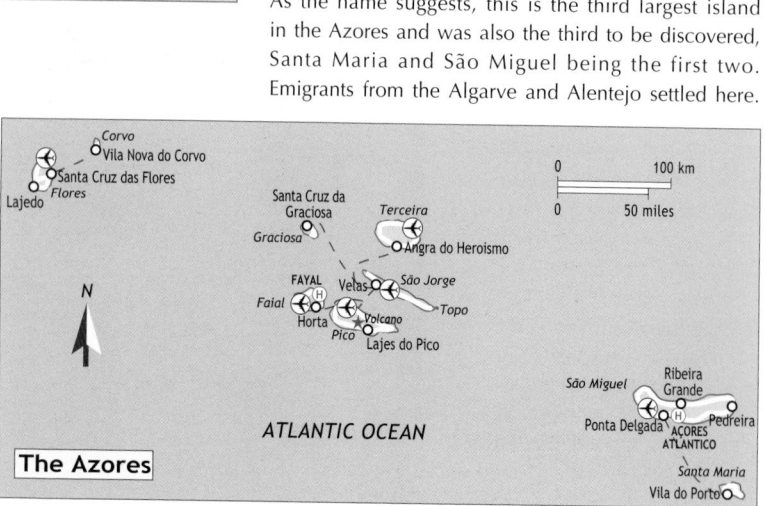

The port of **Angra do Heroismo** was once the political, religious and economic centre of the Azores and has been awarded World Heritage status by UNESCO. The **Old Town** displays Brazilian and American as well as Portuguese influences in its architecture. Unfortunately, it was very badly damaged by an earthquake in 1980 but has been painstakingly restored.

Above: *A ready smile from a village girl.*

Graciosa ★★

The port of Santa Cruz is an attractive town, while the countryside is dotted with **windmills**. Vineyards and maize fields dominate the scenery. The cave of **Furna do Enxofre** is in the middle of a volcanic **caldera**; a spiral staircase leads down into the depths of a chasm where a lake of hot sulphurous water bubbles and boils.

Faial ★★

This is known as the 'blue' island because of the great drifts of hydrangeas which flower here. The capital and only town, **Horta**, is named after an early Dutch settler, Josse van Huerter. The marina is a popular port of call for transatlantic yachts and there's a lively cosmopolitan scene here based around Café Peter. Horta is also a centre for **whale-watching trips**.

Capelinhos, the volcano in the far west of the island, only emerged from the sea in 1957 and joined itself to the mainland. You can walk among the stark solidified **lava flows**, see houses which were buried in ash, and trace the progress of the eruption in a small museum. By contrast the vast crater, or **caldeira**, in the centre of the island is a nature reserve covered in lush vegetation.

PICNIC PROVISIONS

Go to the supermarket and get all the ingredients you need for a memorable picnic; alternatively, shop locally at the market, greengrocers, bakery and *charcuteria* – a delicatessen specializing in cold meats. Here you can buy cold roast chicken, spicy *chouriço* sausage, local cheeses and cartons of prepared salad. If you don't know the name for something, just point and say *'Queria aquilo'* (I'd like that). With some fruit and a bottle of local wine you're all set!

Above: *Beautiful flowers grow in profusion on the fertile soil.*

Pico ★★★

Pico lies 7km (4 miles) east of Faial and is home to the highest mountain in Portugal, the **Pico volcano** which rises to 2351m (7713ft). It's a perfect cone which is snow-capped in winter. Keen walkers can ascend the volcano and, on a clear day, enjoy the magnificent panorama from the summit; it's a round trip of approximately eight hours of tough hiking. There is a **whaling museum** at Lajes do Pico, which is also a base for whale-watching excursions by boat.

São Jorge ★★

This cigar-shaped small island is a haven of rural tranquillity. On the coast *fajãs* (flat areas where cliffs have collapsed) are fertile **orchards**; cows graze in the interior and the island is well known for its **cheeses**. There are also many excellent walks here.

Flores ★★

The name gives a hint to this small island's claim to fame. The most westerly island in the archipelago, it is rugged, thinly populated and covered in **wild flowers**. Its luxuriant vegetation is due to its high rainfall – it rains on average 300 days a year. There are seven crater lakes, deep gorges, fast-flowing trout streams and striking basalt rock formations.

Corvo ★

The smallest island in the archipelago is Corvo. It lies a few kilometres north of Flores; there are daily excursions by boat in summer. The island's 400 inhabitants live in the small port of **Vila Nova do Corvo**. Most visitors make an excursion by jeep or on foot to the **caldera** situated in the hilly interior, which contains two blue lakes dotted with islands.

The Islands: Madeira and the Azores at a Glance

BEST TIMES TO VISIT

Winter is the peak season for Madeira because of its mild climate; hotels often charge less in summer. You can swim in the sea all year, though the Atlantic is warmer in **summer**. The Azores are popular in summer when the weather is warm and dry. However, the mountains may be misty any time of year. From **October** to **April** there can be fog and damp weather. Humidity is high year-round; pack rain wear and layers if you intend to go walking in the mountains or take boat trips.

GETTING THERE

Direct flights go to Madeira from England, Germany and some other northern European countries. **TAP Air Portugal** has several flights a day from Lisbon to both Madeira and the Azores. There are a few flights a week from Madeira to the Azores. There are inter-island connections around the Azores, with turbo prop aircraft flying regular shuttles and also **boat** transfers between the islands.

GETTING AROUND

Madeira has a bus service but it is not very frequent. In the Azores, use taxis. Car hire here is rather expensive; Madeira's prices are more reasonable. Madeira has lots of hotels and apartment accommodation, particularly in the Funchal area.

WHERE TO STAY

LUXURY
Reid's Palace, Estrada Monumental 139, Funchal, tel: 291 717 171, fax: 291 717 177. www.reidspalace.com On seafront, known for its teas and formal dinners.
Cliff Bay, Estrada Monumental 147, Funchal, tel: 291 707 700, fax: 291 762 525. Modern five-star property with excellent sports facilities. www.portobay.pt

MID-RANGE
Quinta do Furão, Achada do Gramacho, 9230 Santana, tel: 291 570 100, www.quintado furao.com Modern, on north coast wine estate, pool.

Azores
Accommodation is limited – book in July and August.

MID-RANGE
Hotel Açores Atlantico, Avenida Infante D Henrique, 9500 Ponta Delgada, São Miguel, tel: 296 302 200, www.bensaude.pt Seafront four-star, modern, efficient
Hotel Fayal, Rua Consul Dabney, 9900 Horta, Faial,

tel: 292 292 181, fax: 292 292 081. Four-star, pool, tennis.

TOURS AND EXCURSIONS

Madeira
Blandy Travel, Avenida Zarco 2, Funchal, tel: 291 200 620.

Azores
Dive Azores, Rua Médico Avalar 13, Horta Faial, tel: 912 585 803, www.dive-centers. net Diving, whale watching.
Aventour, Parque de Campismo da Calheta, São Jorge, tel: 295 416 424, www.aventour-net.com Jeep safaris, riding, hiking, kayaking.

USEFUL CONTACTS

Tourist Offices
Azores Regional Tourist Authority, Largo Almirante Dunn, Ponta Delgada, tel: 296 288 082, www.visit azores.org
Madeira Tourist Office, Palácio Foz, Praça dos Restauradores, 1250 Lisbon, tel: 21 346 9113.
Madeira Tourist Office, Avenida Arriaga 16, 9000 Funchal, tel: 291 211 902, www.madeiratourism.org

FUNCHAL	J	F	M	A	M	J	J	A	S	O	N	D
AVERAGE TEMP. °C	16	16	16	17	18	19	21	22	22	21	18	17
AVERAGE TEMP. °F	60	60	60	63	65	66	71	72	72	71	65	63
HOURS OF SUN DAILY	5	6	6	7	7	7	8	8	8	7	5	5
RAINFALL mm	100	90	70	40	20	10	–	–	20	70	110	80
RAINFALL ins.	3.9	3.5	2.7	1.6	0.8	0.4	–	–	0.8	2.7	4.3	3.1
DAYS OF RAINFALL	15	12	9	7	4	2	–	–	4	9	15	12

Travel Tips

Tourist Information

The Portuguese National Tourist Office is now part of an umbrella promotional organization called **ICEP** – Investimentos, Comércio e Turismo de Portugal.

Main Overseas Offices:

UK: 11 Belgrave Square, London SW1X 8PP, tel: 0845 355 1212;

Ireland: 54 Dawson Street, Dublin 2, tel: (01) 670 9133, email: info@icep.ie

South Africa: 4th Floor, Sunnyside Ridge, Sunnyside Drive, PO Box 2473, Johannesburg 2193, tel: (011) 484 3487, fax: (011) 484 5416;

Canada: 60 Bloor Street West, Suite 1005, Toronto M4W 3B8, tel: (416) 921 7376, email: icep.toronto@icep.pt; 2075 University-Suite 1206, Montreal H3A 2L1, tel: (514) 282 1264, fax: (514) 499 1450;

USA: 590 Fifth Avenue, 4th Floor, New York 10036, tel: (212) 354 4403, email: tourism@portugal.org; 88 Kearny Street, Suite 1770, San Francisco 94108, tel: (415) 391 7080, fax: (415) 391 7147.

In Lisbon ICEP's HQ is: Palacio Foz, Praça dos Restauradores, 1200 Lisbon, tel: 21 346 3314; www.visitportugalinsite.com Open daily 09:00–20:00. Here you can obtain information about the rest of Portugal; the Lisbon Tourist Board has a desk here where you can get local information and buy a Lisboa Card. For general information about the country, visit: www.portugal.org (www.portugal insite.com is also useful).

Entry Requirements

Visitors from European Union countries, as well as those from Australia, New Zealand, the USA and Canada, only need a **valid passport** to enter Portugal. South Africans require a **visa**; visitors of other nationalities are advised to check the current requirements before travel. For stays of more than 90 days a residency permit is required. EU visitors can arrange this locally, but other nationalities may have to leave Portugal and then re-enter the country.

Embassies and Consulates in Lisbon:

Australia: Avenida da Liberdade 198, tel: 21 3101 500;

Great Britain: Rua de São Barnardo 33, tel: 21 312 4000;

Canada: Avenida da Liberdade 196, tel: 21 3164 600;

Ireland: Rua da Imprensa a Estrela 1, tel: 21 3929 440;

New Zealand: Avenida Antonio Aguiar 122, tel: 21 350 9690;

South Africa: Avenida Luis Bivar 10, tel: 21 3304 217;

USA: Avenida das Forças Armadas, tel: 21 727 3300.

Customs

The duty-free allowance for travellers aged over 17 arriving from a non-EU country is: 200 cigarettes or 100 cigarillos or 50 cigars or 250g of rolling tobacco; 1 litre spirits or 2 litres wine; 250ml perfume. If arriving from the EU you can bring in any amount of duty-paid goods provided you can prove they are for your personal use and not for resale. Current guidelines suggest 800 cigarettes, 10 litres spirits and 90 litres wine but as prices for all these are low in Portugal it is hardly worth the bother; rather buy them in Portugal if you're going to another EU nation.

Health Requirements

Yellow fever certificate needed if arriving from an infected area. Travellers are advised to take out appropriate **travel insurance** policies which cover any emergency medical care.

Getting There

By Air: Portugal's international airports are Lisbon, Oporto, Faro and Funchal. **TAP Air Portugal** flies to Lisbon from most major European cities, plus selected routings from North and South America and Africa. Many of these routes are mirrored by national airlines, e.g. the UK's **British Airways** and Brazil's **Varig**. Oporto, Faro and Funchal are served exclusively by European flights. **Portugalia**, Portugal's second airline, concentrates on the domestic market but has international flights from cities such as Manchester and Turin. There are year-round charter flights to Faro from northern Europe and these can be cheaper than scheduled fares, though you have to stay for a minimum of a week. The UK is a particularly good source of low-cost flights, with deals available to both Lisbon and Faro.

By Road: Some three dozen roads cross the Spanish border. The best entry points on better roads from north to south are: Valença do Minho, Feces de Abajo, Vilar Formoso, Elvas, Vila Verde de Ficalho and Vila Real. From northern Spain the quickest route is via Salamanca; from Madrid via Badajoz and Seville is just 153km (95 miles) from Vila Real in the Algarve.

By Bus: Express bus services go to Lisbon from London, Paris, Hamburg, Hanover and Düsseldorf, less frequent connections to Oporto and Faro. From Spain you can travel from Madrid to Oporto and Lisbon, from Barcelona to Lisbon, from Malaga to Lisbon and from Seville to Faro.

By Rail: Two main routes into Portugal are Paris to northern Spain (change for Oporto and Lisbon) and Paris to Madrid (pick up the Lisbon-bound **Talgo Lusitania**). It takes 20 hours from Paris to Lisbon and ten hours from Madrid to Lisbon. If you travel by rail a lot, enquire about a **rail pass**; there are different varieties for European residents, non-Europeans, those aged under 26 and senior citizens.

What to Pack

From **June to September** pack light summer clothes. In **April/May** and **October/ November** add a jacket and a few layers to cope with cool weather. In winter and early spring you will need a mixture of cotton and warmer clothes. A lightweight rain jacket is useful outside high summer. Bathing suits should not be worn in **town**; however, shorts are worn around resorts. Women will attract less attention in cities and **rural areas** by wearing a skirt or trousers. Shops are well stocked and if you forget some essential item you should be able to replace it.

Money Matters

Currency: Like most of Western Europe, Portugal has adopted the euro, so you don't need to change money

if you are arriving from Spain. Exchange rates do fluctuate, but a euro is roughly equivalent in value to the US dollar. The euro notes in circulation are in 5, 10, 20, 50, 100, 200 and 500 euro denominations, and there are 1 and 2 euro coins, as well as cents (100 cents to the euro) with values ranging from 1 to 50.

Exchange: Normal banking hours are from 08:30–15:00 Monday to Friday. The desk marked *câmbios* is the place where you can change traveller's cheques; don't forget your passport. Traveller's cheques may also be exchanged at the reception desk of many hotels and in bureaux de change. In most towns, you're never far from an automatic teller machine (ATM) where you can withdraw currency 24 hours a day using a debit or credit card. All the major credit cards are widely accepted in shops, restaurants and garages. If you're going off the beaten track, stock up on cash.

Tipping: Restaurant and hotel bills include a service charge, but a tip of 5–10% is normal for good service; the same applies to taxis. For drinks and snacks leave some loose change. Hotel porters and petrol pump attendants will also appreciate a small tip.

Accommodation

Hotels range from one to five stars. *Estalagems* and *albergarias* are inns, *see* www.solaresdeportugal.pt *Residencials* are hotels offering only bed and breakfast, not evening meals; guesthouses are called *pensões* (singular *pensão*). These are graded from one to three stars and are normally reasonably priced, clean and comfortable. All but the most basic offer private bathrooms. Rooms are widely available to rent in private houses; look for a sign *quartos* in the window. There are 23 **youth hostels** in Portugal, part of the Hostelling International network.

Camping can be an excellent way to enjoy the countryside at very reasonable prices, particularly in summer when you can rely on good weather. Larger sites have pools and restaurants. Local tourist offices can provide details, or check out the following websites: www.roteiro-campista.pt and www.orbitur.pt

The *Turismo de Habitação* scheme gives grants to owners of houses of historic interest to provide accommodation for guests. The similar *Turismo Rural* and *Afroturismo* schemes also include simpler farmhouses. All tend to be known collectively as Turihab and include self-catering cottages as well as B&B. Contact tourist offices for details, or visit www.turihab.pt and www.manorhouses.com *Pousadas* are government-run hotels located in historic buildings such as castles and convents or modern properties in scenic areas. Exclusive and expensive, they are run to high standards and include a certain amount of Portuguese charm. There are over 60 scattered around the country; you can get details from tourist offices or www.pousadas.pt

Eating Out

As well as *restaurante* signs you may see *tasca* (tavern), *cervejaria* (simple dishes), *marisqueria* (seafood specialities) or *churrasqueira* (grills and barbecues). **Breakfast** is normally coffee and bread. **Lunch** is served from 13:00–15:00, dinner 19:00–22:00. Shellfish is invariably the most expensive thing on the menu and is often marked PV, short for *preço variavel*, when the price per kilo is quoted at current market rates. Set menus are good value, as is the *prato del dia* or dish of the day. Portions are large; you can ask for a *meia dose* or half portion. House wine (*vinho da casa*) is normally good and very cheap.

Snacks include *sandes* (sandwiches) and *tosta mista* (toasted cheese and ham). For starters, home-made soups are excellent. **Fish** is widely available, and good meat choices include *leitao asado* (roast suckling pig), *coelho* (rabbit), *cabrito* (kid), *borrego* (lamb) and *frango* (chicken). **Vegetarians** don't seem to have much choice beyond salad, chips, omelette and cheese; even the soups are often flavoured with meat broth. **Desserts** are limited; for a good choice of cakes and concoctions head to a *pastelaria*.

Transport

Car Hire: You need a valid domestic or international **licence** to hire a car and you must be over 23. **Car hire** is relatively inexpensive and all

From	To	Multiply By
Millimetres	Inches	0.0394
Metres	Yards	1.0936
Metres	Feet	3.281
Kilometres	Miles	0.6214
Square kilometres	Square miles	0.386
Hectares	Acres	2.471
Litres	Pints	1.760
Kilograms	Pounds	2.205
Tonnes	Tons	0.984

CONVERSION CHART

To convert Celsius to Fahrenheit: x 9 ÷ 5 + 32

major international companies are represented along with plenty of local firms. You can obtain more competitive rates by pre-booking a car with your flight rather than on arrival.
Road Rules: Driving is on the right side of the road; **speed limits** are 50kph (32mph) in town, 90kph (55mph) outside built-up areas, 100kph (62mph) on national roads (look for N or EN prefix) and 120kph (75mph) on motorways. Roads have improved vastly thanks to EU subsidies. In remote rural areas keep the **petrol** tank topped up. Most hire cars take unleaded (*sem chumbo*) petrol. The standard of driving is appalling and the **accident fatality rate** is the highest in Europe so hire the best car you can afford. Grade C is the minimum to consider; try go higher. Mild mannered and relaxed most of the time, the Portuguese turn into demons behind the wheel.
Overtaking three abreast and on blind corners and hills is common. If you are about to overtake, always check over your left shoulder to make sure the car behind is not about to overtake you. On motorways you could be overtaking a lorry when a Porsche or BMW appears from nowhere in the fast lane at 200kph (125 mph). Three notoriously dangerous roads are the EN125 in the Algarve, the A5 from Lisbon to Cascais, and the IP5 from Guarda to Aveiro. In town, **indicating** at roundabouts and intersections is uncommon. In rural areas drive carefully and watch for **animals** or tractors

blocking the road. **Drunk driving** laws exist (the litmus test is .5g/litre or more) but are not always adhered to; however, the penalties can be harsh. The *Automovel Clube de Portugal* (www.acp.pt) has arrangements with major national motoring organizations; the **emergency** help number is tel: 707 509 510.
Buses: There are three main types of service: fast direct **expressos** between cities, fast regional **rapidas**, and local **carreiras** which stop every few minutes. Buy express tickets from www.rede-expressos.pt or the local station.
Trains: Generally cheaper and slower than buses. Slow regional trains are marked **R** on timetables; faster inter-regional trains **IR** and express services are called *rapido* or *intercidade* – look for **IC**. For timetables, contact Comboios de Portugal (tel: 808 208 208; www.cp.pt).
Taxis: There are ranks in all towns and also radio taxis.
Fares from airports are set; look for a list of prices at the cab rank or check with the tourist information kiosk. Cabs are metered so if you are planning on a longer journey, agree to a price with the driver beforehand.
Air: TAP Air Portugal and Portugalia operate regular services between Lisbon, Oporto and Faro; TAP also has flights to and from Madeira and the Azores.

Business Hours

Office hours are generally 09:00–13:00 and 15:00–

ROAD SIGNS

Abrande • Slow Down
Atenção • Attention
Cuidado • Caution
Curva perigrosa • Dangerous bend
De prioridade • Give way
Desvio • Diversion
Espere • Wait
Estacionamento proibido • No parking
Obras na estrada • Road works
Pare • Stop
Parque de estacionamento • Car park
Passagem proibida • no entry
Perigo • Danger

17:00 Monday–Friday. Shops are open from 09:00–13:00 and 15:00–18:00. Some close on Saturday afternoons.

Communications

Post Offices are open 09:00–18:00 Monday–Friday. Stamps are also sold in kiosks and many general stores.
Telephone calls can be made from coin- or card-operated phone boxes. Phone cards (*cartão telefonico*) are available from newsagents and kiosks. For a local call you will need to dial the **area code**, which is now prefixed by a 2 rather than a 0. For example, if you are in Lisbon and calling a Lisbon number, you will still have to dial 21. Mobile phone network coverage is very good.

Electricity

Voltage is 220/380 volts at a frequency of 50 Hertz. Standard European two-pin plugs are used.

GOOD READING

Buck, Paul (2002) *Lisbon* (Signal).
Kaplan, Marion (1998) *The Portuguese* (Penguin).
Saramago, José, translated by Nick Caistor and Amanda Hopkinson (2002) *Journey to Portugal* (Harvill Press).
Anderson, Jean (1994) *The Food of Portugal* (William Morrow).
Birmingham, David (2003) *A Concise History of Portugal* (Cambridge).
Russell, Peter (2001) *Prince Henry the Navigator* (Yale Nota Bene).
Russell, A J R (1998) *The Portuguese Empire 1415–1808* (John Hopkins University).
Mayson, Richard (2003) *The Wines and Vineyards of Portugal* (Mitchell Beazley).
Vieira, Edite (2000) *The Taste of Portugal* (Grub Street).
Saraiva, José Hermano (1997) *Portugal: A Companion History* (Carcanet).

Weights and Measures

Portugal uses the metric system.

Health Precautions

Tap **water** is drinkable but bottled water is also available. **Mosquitoes** can be a problem in summer. The **sun** is strong so use protection cream; if active, drink plenty of water to guard against dehydration.

Personal Safety

The crime rate is generally low in rural Portugal but Lisbon and tourist resorts are targeted by professional **thieves**. Keep bags and wallets secure when on the street and don't carry valuables around with you. Bags and cameras should be locked away in the boot of your car. Women should not experience particular problems but should be careful about walking alone at night and accepting lifts from strangers.

Emergencies

In case of emergencies dial **112** and ask the operator for **police** (*policia*), **fire services** (*bombeiros*) or **ambulance** (*ambulancia*). Try to enlist the aid of one of the locals if you don't speak any Portuguese.

Etiquette

Courteous greetings such as *bom dia,* (good morning), *boa tarde* (good afternoon) and *boa noite* (good night) are the norm. Beyond this the Portuguese are informal but good manners are expected of visitors; rude or aggressive behaviour is frowned on, as is excessive drinking.

Health Services

All towns have a **health centre** (*centro de saude*) and the cities have larger hospitals. There are also private doctors and hospitals. For minor ailments visit a **pharmacy** (*farmacia*). Public health services are at best mediocre by European standards; however, a decent travel insurance policy will enable you to get good-quality private treatment. Lisbon's British Hospital, tel: (21) 395 5067, has English-speaking staff.

Time Difference

Portugal is on GMT in **winter** and GMT plus one hour in **summer** (an hour earlier than Spain and the rest of Western Europe, excluding the UK). The Azores are two hours earlier than mainland Portugal.

INDEX

Note: Numbers in **bold** indicate photographs